D1237096

AXE-AGE, WOLF-AGE

AXE-AGE, WOLF-AGE
A selection from the Norse Myths

Retold by
KEVIN CROSSLEY-HOLLAND

Illustrated by
Hannah Firmin

ANDRE DEUTSCH

First published 1985 by
André Deutsch Limited
105 Great Russell Street London WC1

British Library Cataloguing in Publication Data

Crossley-Holland, Kevin
  Axe-age, wolf-age
  1. Mythology, Norse—Juvenile literature
  I. Title   II. Firmin, Hannah
  293'.13   PZ8.1

  ISBN 0-233-97688-4

Typeset in 12pt Monotype Joanna
by Merrion Letters
119 Hackford Road London SW9
Printed by Ebenezer Baylis & Son Ltd
The Trinity Press, Worcester, and London

for Katharine Findlay
my god-daughter

CONTENTS

Hail to the speaker and him who listens! May whoever learns these words prosper because of them! Hail to those who listen!

Havamal

FOREWORD

W HEN Odin, ruler of the gods and of all creation, sits in the high seat in his hall Valhalla, he can see everything in the nine worlds. Mountains and seas and shining fields, men and women and children and monsters, giants, dwarfs, with his one eye he can see them all. But Odin cannot bear to be out of things. His blood races; he longs to test life's winds and tides for himself. Before long, he leaves his high seat and his hall, and hurries down to one place or another, hungry for some happening.

Forty generations ago, the Vikings were rather like this. They were like the restless, eager, sometimes cruel, powerful god whom they created and worshipped. They conquered Scotland and Ireland and half of England, settled in the Low Countries and northern France (Norman means North-man or Norseman) and raided towns in Spain and Portugal and Italy; they worked their way through Russia to the Black Sea and Constantinople, the Caspian Sea and Baghdad; and in their superb and graceful ships, they went to Iceland and Greenland and Newfoundland and the eastern seaboard of the United States. They were hit-and-run raiders, mercenaries, merchants, settlers, lawgivers, a colonial people as dominant in their own time as were the British in the nineteenth century and the Americans and Russians today.

Wherever they went, the Vikings took with them their own customs and beliefs. They believed, for example, that our world (Midgard) was sandwiched between two other levels. The top level is called Asgard, realm of the gods, and it is linked to Midgard by a flaming rainbow bridge called Bifrost. Not only humans inhabit Midgard but over the mountains in the east there are warlike giants, and in caves and potholes live unpleasant, greedy dwarfs. Nine days' ride northwards and downwards from Midgard lies the third level of Niflheim, world of the dead, a place of bitter cold and unending night. Why and how the three levels and nine worlds of this universe came into being, and who lives in them, are thrillingly described in the first myth in this book.

Why and how and who? These questions lie at the heart of myth. Why does the sun appear in the morning and disappear at night? How is it that thunder sounds as it does sound? And who gave countries and oceans their individual shapes? Through stories that are racy and fanciful and stirring, and through colourful characters (many of whom reappear from myth to myth, giving the cycle the appearance of linked short stories), the Norse myths provide explanations which enable us to see the old world around us with new eyes.

We all know, for instance, that spring and summer follow winter; and that if they did not it would be the worse for us. But why do the seasons turn? You, and perhaps I, could explain things in scientific terms by describing how Sun and Earth come closer together before drawing apart again. But the Vikings knew little or nothing of this. They had their own explanation.

They said that Freyr, god of fertility, was almost blinded by the beauty of the ice-giantess Gerd:

> When she raised her arms to close the hall doors, the dome of
> the sky and the sea surrounding the earth at once grew brighter.
> Because of her, all the worlds were hidden in a flash of brilliant,
> icy light.

Freyr falls in love with Gerd. He is the god of sun and rain and harvests; she represents all that is frozen and cannot grow. At first Gerd will have nothing to do with Freyr. But the god becomes more heated and more insistent. And what happens when sun meets ice? Eventually ice melts. And because of their union, as shown in the eighth myth, crops of barley grow. This myth is not more true or less true than a scientific explanation of the seasons and their turning; it is simply a different way of seeing.

As you might expect, the myths tell us much about the Vikings — their spirit and confidence and wit, their curiosity and bravery, their clannish loyalty and generosity, their cunning and ruthlessness and fatalism. Here or there a word or act may seem outlandish or cruel, but it is not right to chew up the original simply because our own age disapproves of such attitudes. The Vikings would doubtless have found some twentieth-century attitudes impossible to like or even understand. But like all great imaginative literature, the myths are not imprisoned in their own time and place; they tell us of their makers but they also tell us a lot about ourselves — our own deep longings and fears.

In retelling these myths, first published in my book *The Norse Myths*, I closely followed the two thirteenth-century Icelandic sources (the thirty-four poems of the *Elder Edda* and Snorri Sturluson's *Prose Edda*) on which we depend for much the greater part of our knowledge of Norse mythology, but did not hesitate to develop hints, flesh out dramatic situations and add snatches of dialogue. Drawing on a wide variety of sources and my own observation of Iceland, I tried to portray some descriptive background to the myths – a background the original audience would have taken for granted. And I found it right to use good, blunt words with Anglo-Saxon roots wherever I could do so. Since there is no 'right' order for the myths, which were the product of countless people, times and places, I simply attempted to find a psychologically satisfying sequence, leading inescapably towards Ragnarok, that reduced con-tradictions and chronological inconsistencies to a minimum. In re-printing twenty-two myths for this edition, I have followed the text of *The Norse Myths* except, here and there, to omit an insignificant name, or to hone some sound or meaning.

Walsham-le-Willows
January 1984

THE CREATION

BURNING ice, biting flame; that is how life began.

In the south is a realm called Muspell. That region flickers with dancing flames. It seethes and it shines. No one can endure it except those born into it. Black Surt is there; he sits on the furthest reach of that land, brandishing a flaming sword; he is already waiting for the end when he will rise and savage the gods and whelm the whole world with fire.

In the north is a realm called Niflheim. It is packed with ice and covered with vast sweeps of snow. In the heart of that region lies the spring Hvergelmir and that is the source of eleven rivers named the Elivagar.

Between these realms there once stretched a huge and seeming emptiness; this was Ginnungagap. The rivers that sprang from Hvergelmir streamed into the void. The yeasty venom in them thickened and congealed like slag, and the rivers turned into ice. That venom also spat out drizzle – an unending dismal hagger that, as soon as it settled, turned into rime. So it went on until all the northern part of Ginnungagap was heavy with layers of ice and hoar frost, a desolate place haunted by gusts and skuthers of wind.

Just as the northern part was frozen, the southern was molten and glowing, but the middle of Ginnungagap was as mild as hanging air on a summer evening. There, the warm breath drifting north from Muspell met the rime from Niflheim; it touched it and played over it, and the ice began to thaw and drip. Life quickened in those drops, and they took the form of a giant. He was called Ymir.

Ymir was a frost giant; he was evil from the first. While he slept, he began to sweat. A man and woman grew out of the ooze under his left armpit, and one of his legs fathered a son on the other leg. Ymir was the forefather of all the frost giants.

As more of the ice in Ginnungagap melted, the fluid took the form of a cow. She was called Audumla. Ymir fed off the four rivers of milk that coursed from her teats, and Audumla fed off the ice itself. She licked the salty blocks and by the evening of the first day a man's hair had come out of the ice. Audumla licked more and by the evening of the second day a man's head had come. Audumla licked again and by the evening of the third day the whole man had come. His name was Buri.

Buri was tall and strong and good-looking. In time he had a son called Bor and Bor married a daughter of one of the frost giants. Her name was Bestla and she mothered three children, all of them sons. The first was Odin, the second was Vili, and the third was Ve.

All this was in the beginning, before there were waves of sand, the sea's cool waves, waving grass. There was no earth and no heaven above; only Muspell and Niflheim and, between them, Ginnungagap.

The three sons of Bor had no liking for Ymir and the growing gang of unruly, brutal frost giants; as time went on, they grew to hate them. At last they attacked Ymir and killed him. His wounds were like springs; so much blood streamed from them, and so fast, that the flood drowned all the frost giants except one called Bergelmir and his wife. They embarked in their boat – it was made out of a hollowed tree trunk – and rode on a tide of gore.

Odin and Vili and Ve hoisted the body of the dead frost giant onto their shoulders and carted it to the middle of Ginnungagap. That is where they made the world from his body. They shaped the earth from Ymir's flesh and the mountains from his unbroken bones; from his teeth and jaws and the fragments of his shattered bones they made rocks and boulders and stones.

Odin and Vili and Ve used the welter of blood to make landlocked lakes and to make the sea. After they had formed the earth, they laid the rocking ocean in a ring right round it. And it is so wide that most men would dismiss the very idea of crossing it.

Then the three brothers raised Ymir's skull and made the sky from it and placed it so that its four corners reached to the ends of the earth. They set a dwarf under each corner, and their names are East and West and North and South. Then Odin and Vili and Ve seized on the sparks and glowing embers from the southern realm of Muspell and called them sun and moon and stars; they put them high in Ginnungagap to light heaven above and earth below. In this way the brothers gave each star its proper place; some were fixed in the sky, others were free to follow the paths appointed for them.

The earth was round and lay within the ring of the deep sea. Along the strand the sons of Bor marked out tracts of land and gave them to the frost giants and the rock giants; they called that land Jotunheim, and there the giants settled and remained. They were so hostile that the three brothers built an enclosure further inland around a vast area of the earth. They shaped it out of Ymir's eyebrows, and called it Midgard. The sun warmed the stones in the earth there, and the ground was green with sprouting leeks. The sons of Bor used Ymir's brains as well; they flung them up into the air and turned them into every kind of cloud.

One day, Odin and Vili and Ve were striding along the frayed edge of the land, where the earth meets the sea. They came across two fallen trees with their roots ripped out of the ground; one was an ash, the other an elm. Then the sons of Bor raised them and made from them the first man and woman. Odin breathed into them the spirit of life; Vili offered them sharp wits and feeling hearts; and Ve gave them the gifts of hearing and sight. The man was called Ask and the woman Embla and they were given Midgard to live in. All the families and nations and races of men are descended from them.

One of the giants living in Jotunheim had a daughter called Night who was as dark eyed, dark haired and swarthy as the rest of her family. She married three times and the son of her third marriage was called Day. Like all his father's side of the family, Day was radiant and fair of face.

Then Odin took Night and her son Day, sat them in horse-drawn chariots, and set them in the sky to ride round the world every two half-days. Night leads the way and her horse is frosty-maned. Day's horse has a gleaming mane that lights up sky and earth alike.

A man called Mundilfari living in Midgard had two children and they were so beautiful that he called his son Moon and his daughter Sun. Odin and his brothers and their offspring, the Aesir, were angered at such daring. They snatched away both children and placed them in the sky to guide the chariots of the sun and moon.

Moon leads the way. He guides the moon on its path and decides when he will wax and wane. He does not travel alone, as you can see if you look into the sky; for Moon in turn plucked two children from Midgard. They were just walking away from the well carrying between them a cask of water on a pole when Moon swooped down and carried them off.

Sun follows behind. One of her horses is called Arvak because he rises so early, and the other Alsvid because he is immensely swift and strong. The Aesir inserted iron-cold bellows under their shoulder-blades to keep them cool. Sun always seems to be in a great hurry, and that is because she is chased by Skoll, the wolf who is always snapping and growling close behind her. In the end he will catch her. And the wolf that races in front of Sun is called Hati; he is after Moon and will run him down in the end. Both wolves are the sons of an aged giantess who lived in Iron Wood, east of Midgard.

After the sons of Bor had made the first man and woman, and set Night and Day, Moon and Sun in the sky, they remembered the maggots that had squirmed and swarmed in Ymir's flesh and crawled out over the earth. Then they gave them wits and the shape of men, but they live under the hills and mountains in rocky chambers and grottoes and caverns. These man-like maggots are called dwarfs.

So the earth was fashioned and filled with men and giants and dwarfs, surrounded by the sea and covered by the sky. Then the sons of Bor built their own realm of Asgard – a mighty stronghold, a place of green plains and shining palaces high over Midgard. The two regions were linked by Bifrost, a flaming rainbow bridge; it was made of three colours with magic and great skill, and it is wonderfully strong. All the Aesir crossed over and settled in Asgard. Odin, Allfather, is the oldest and greatest of them all; there are twelve divine gods and twelve divine goddesses, and a great assembly of other Aesir. And this was the beginning of all that has happened, remembered or forgotten, in the regions of the world.

And all that has happened, and all the regions of the world, lie under the branches of the ash Yggdrasill, greatest and best of trees, axis of the world. It soars over all that is; its three roots delve into Asgard and Jotunheim and Niflheim, and there is a spring under each. Odin gave one eye for a single draught from the spring of Mimir in Jotunheim; he won immense knowledge there and with it the thirst for yet greater wisdom. A hawk and eagle sit in the branches of Yggdrasill, a squirrel whisks up and down it, deer leap within it and nibble at it, goats tug and tear at its tender shoots, a dragon devours it. The three Norns live near by, Fate and Being and Necessity. They shape the life of each man from his first day to his last. And every day they sprinkle water on the branches of the tree. Yggdrasill gives life to itself, it gives life to the unborn. The winds whirl round it and Yggdrasill croons or groans. Yggdrasill always was and is and will be.

THE BUILDING OF
ASGARD'S WALL

THE gods argued; they deceived one another and angered one another. Then Odin cast his spear, and that was the beginning of the first war in the world.

The towering wall round Asgard was soon reduced to ruins. And long after the gods had grown weary of war, and settled their differences, and declared a truce, that is how it remained: a ring of rubble, deserted, the home of eagles and ravens.

The gods were anxious that the wall should be rebuilt, so that Asgard would be safe from evil-doers, but none were eager to take the heavy burden of rebuilding on their own shoulders. This is how matters stood for some time until, one day, a solitary figure on horseback cantered over the trembling rainbow, and was stopped by Heimdall, watchman of the Gods.

'I've a plan to put to the gods,' said the man.

'You can put it to me,' said Heimdall warmly. He had felt curious as he watched this man approach from a hundred miles off, and smiled, showing his gold teeth.

'I'll put it to all the gods if I put it at all,' said the man from his saddle. 'The goddesses also may be interested.'

Heimdall showed his teeth again in a less friendly manner and directed the man across the Plain of Ida to the great hall Gladsheim

So the gods and goddesses gathered in Gladsheim. Their visitor tied up his stallion and stepped forward under the shining roof, to the middle of the hall. He was surrounded by Odin and the twelve leading gods, each sitting in his high place, and by a throng of gods and goddesses.

Odin eyed him piercingly. 'We are all here at Heimdall's bidding. What do you have to say?'

'Only this,' said the man. 'I'll rebuild your wall round Asgard.'

There was a stir in Gladsheim as the gods and goddesses realised there must be rather more to the builder than met the eye.

'The wall will be much stronger and higher than before,' said the builder. 'So strong and high that it will be impregnable. Asgard will be secure against the rock giants and the frost giants even if they barge their way into Midgard.'

'However,' said Odin, aware that conditions would soon follow.

'I'll need eighteen months,' said the builder. 'Eighteen months from the day I begin.'

'That may not be impossible,' said Odin, the Alert One.

'It is essential,' said the builder.

'And your price?' asked Odin slowly.

'I was coming to that,' said the builder. 'Freyja as my wife.'

The beautiful goddess sat bolt upright and as she moved her necklace and her golden brooches and armbands and the gold thread in her clothing glittered and flashed. None but Odin could look directly at her, Freyja, fairest of goddesses. And as she sat erect, the outraged gods all around her were shouting, or waving their arms, deriding the builder, dismissing the builder.

'That's impossible,' shouted Odin. 'Let that be an end to it.'

'I'll also be wanting the sun and the moon,' said the builder. 'Freyja, the sun and the moon: that's my price.'

Loki's voice rose out of the hubbub. 'Every idea has its own merits. Don't dismiss it out of hand.'

All the gods and goddesses turned to look at the Sly One, the giant Farbauti's son, and wondered what was passing through the maze of his mind.

'We must give this plan thought,' said Loki reasonably. 'We owe our guest no less.'

So the builder was asked to leave Gladsheim while the gods and goddesses conferred. And when she saw that the gods were no longer ready to dismiss the idea out of hand but wanted to discuss it in earnest, Freyja began to weep tears of gold.

'Don't be so hasty,' Loki said. 'We could turn this plan to our own gain. Supposing we gave this man six months to build the wall . . .'

'He could never build it in that time,' said Heimdall.

'Never,' echoed many of the gods.

'Exactly,' said Loki.

Odin smiled.

'So what would we lose by suggesting it?' said Loki. 'If the builder won't agree, we lose nothing. If he does agree, he's bound to lose.' Loki slapped his sides and rolled his eyes. 'And we'll have half our wall built, free and for nothing.'

Although the gods and goddesses were a little uneasy about taking Loki's advice, they could see no way to fault the Trickster's scheme. Indeed several of them wished they had thought of it themselves.

'Six months!' said Odin, when the builder had come back into Gladsheim. 'If you build the wall within this time, you can have Freyja as your wife, and take the sun and moon too. Six months.'

The builder shook his head, but Odin continued, 'Tomorrow is the first day of winter. You must agree that no one may come to help you. And if any part of the wall is still unfinished on the first day of summer, you forfeit your reward. Those are our terms, and there are none other.'

'Impossible terms,' said the builder, 'and you know it.' He paused and gazed at Freyja. 'But my longing,' he said. 'My longing . . .' He gazed at Freyja again. 'Then at least allow me the help of my stallion Svadilfari.'

'Those are our terms,' said Odin.

'And those are mine,' said the builder.

'Odin, you're too stubborn,' protested Loki.

'And there are none other,' said Odin firmly.

'What's wrong with allowing him the use of his horse?' shouted Loki. 'How can it possibly affect the outcome? If we refuse, there'll be no bargain, and we'll have no part of the wall at all.'

In the end, Loki's argument prevailed. It was agreed that the builder should begin work on the next morning and have the use of his horse. Odin swore oaths to this effect in front of many witnesses, and the builder also asked for safe conduct for as long as he worked on the wall. He said he was anxious in case Thor, who was away in the east fighting trolls at that time, should return home and fail to see matters in the way the other gods had done.

*   *   *

Long before Early Waker and All Swift set off on their journey across the sky, the builder started work. By the light of the new moon, he led Svadilfari down over a sweeping grassy shoulder and past a copse to a place where the bones of the hill were sticking out, chipped and twisted. There were huge hunks and chunks and boulders of rock there, stuff that looked as though it would last as long as time itself. The builder brought with him a loosely-meshed net which he harnessed to his stallion and spread out behind him. Then he began to heave and shove massive slabs on to the net. He gasped and grunted – amongst the gods only Thor could have matched his strength. After some time he had levered and piled up a great mound of rock behind Svadilfari. Then the builder gathered up the net ends in his horny hands, as though he were folding a sheet, and bellowed.

At once Svadilfari bowed his head. He dug his shoes into the earth and began to haul. Mustering his vast strength he dragged the whole quaking mound up the slope. And as day dawned, the builder and his stallion, guffing in the freezing air, brought their load up beside the old broken wall of Asgard.

When the gods and goddesses stirred from their halls, they were astonished and disturbed to see how much rock Svadilfari had hauled up the hill. They watched the mason smash the boulders, and shape them, and set them in place while Svadilfari rested in the shadow of the growing wall; and such was his strength, they began to think that the mason could only be some giant in disguise. But then the gods looked at the great circuit of wall that remained broken; they reassured each other that they had in any case got the best of the bargain.

Winter bared its teeth. The corpse-eating eagle Hraesvelg beat his wings and, outside Asgard, the cold wind whirled. The land was drenched by rainstorms and pelted with hailstones, then draped in snow.

The giant mason and his horse gritted their teeth and worked at the wall. Night after night Svadilfari ploughed the long furrow past the copse to and from the quarry. Day after day the mason went on building. And as the days grew longer, time for the mason, and for the gods, grew shorter.

Three days before the beginning of summer the mason had almost completed the circuit of well cut and well laid stone, a sturdy wall high and strong enough to keep any unwelcome visitor at bay. Only the gateway had still to be built. The gods and goddesses were no more able to keep away from the wall than moths from a flame. They stared at it for the hundredth time; they talked of nothing but the bargain.

Then Odin called a meeting in Gladsheim. The high hall was filled with anxious faces and fretful talk. Freyja was unable to stem her tears – the floor around her was flooded with gold.

Odin raised his spear and his voice over the assembly: 'We must find a way out of this contract,' he shouted. 'Who suggested we should strike this bargain? How did we come to risk such an outcome: Freyja married to a brute of a giant? The sky raped of the sun and the moon so that we shall have to grope about, robbed of light and warmth?' Several gods and then every god looked at Loki, and Odin strode across the hall floor towards him. He took a firm grip on the Trickster's shoulders.

'How was I to know?' protested Loki. 'We all agreed.'

Odin tightened his grip and Loki winced.

'We all agreed!' yelled Loki.

'Who suggested the mason should be allowed to have the use of his horse?' Odin asked. 'You got us into this trouble and you must get us out of it.'

There was a shout of agreement from all the gods.

'Use the warp and weft of your mind, Loki. Weave some plan. Either the mason forfeits his wages or you forfeit your life.' Odin squeezed Loki's flesh and sinews until the Sly One, the Shape Changer, dropped to one knee. 'We'll take it all out of you, bit by bit.'

Loki saw that Odin and the other gods were in deadly earnest. 'I swear,' he said. 'No matter what it costs me, I'll see to it that the builder loses the wager.'

That evening the mason led Svadilfari down towards the quarry with a certain spring in his step. It seemed to him as to the gods and goddesses that he would finish the wall within the agreed time, and win rewards rich not only in themselves but also in the sorrow their loss would bring to the gods. He sang a kind of tune, and small birds took shelter in the gloomy copse and listened to his song. Not only the birds. A young mare pricked up her ears and listened intently. She listened as if her life depended upon it. Then, when Svadilfari and the mason drew close enough, she sprang out of the thicket. She kicked her heels in the air and, in the moonlight, her flanks simmered.

The mare pranced up to Svadilfari. She danced around him and whisked her tail and Svadilfari began to strain at the long rein by which the mason was leading him.

Then the mare whinnied invitingly and headed back towards the copse. Svadilfari started after her with such a thrust that he broke the rein. He galloped behind the mare into the copse, and the mason lumbered after Svadilfari, shouting and cursing.

All night the two horses gambolled, and all night the enraged mason tripped over roots and tree stumps in the half light. He hurled abuses, he chased shadows, and the light had begun to grow green in the east before Svadilfari returned to him.

So no stone was hauled from the quarry that night and the mason had to make do with the little left over from the day before. It was not nearly enough to build the first part of the gateway and he soon knew that he would no longer be able to complete his task in time.

Then the anger churning inside the mason erupted. He burst out of his disguise and stood before the watching gods and goddesses – a towering brute of a rock giant in a towering rage.

Now that the gods knew the builder was indeed a giant, they revoked their oaths about his safe conduct without a second thought, and sent for Thor.

'A trick!' shouted the rock giant. 'Tricked by a gang of gods! A brothel of goddesses!'

Those were the mason's last words. Then Thor paid him his wages, and they were not the sun and the moon. A single blow from the hammer Mjollnir shattered the giant's skull into a thousand fragments and dispatched him to the endless dark of Niflheim.

A number of months passed before Loki the Shape Changer was seen in Asgard again. And when he returned, ambling over Bifrost and blowing a raspberry at the watchman Heimdall, he had a colt in tow. This horse was rather unusual in that he had eight legs. He was a grey and Loki called him Sleipnir.

When Odin saw Sleipnir, he admired the colt greatly.

'Take him!' said Loki. 'I bore him and he'll bear you. You'll find he can outpace Golden and Joyous, Shining and Swift, Silver-maned and Sinewy, Gleaming and Hollow-hoofed, Gold Mane and Light Feet, and outrun whatever horses there are in Jotunheim. No horse will ever be able to keep up with him.'

Odin thanked Loki warmly, and welcomed him back to Asgard.

'On this horse you can go wherever you want,' said Loki. 'He'll gallop over the sea and through the air. What other horse could bear its rider down the long road to the land of the dead, and then bear him back to Asgard again?'

Odin thanked Loki a second time and looked at the Sly One very thoughtfully.

THE RACES OF MEN

LISTEN! Who can hear the sound of grass growing? The sound of wool on a sheep's back, growing?

Who needs less sleep than a bird?

Who is so eagle-eyed that, by day and by night, he can see the least movement a hundred leagues away?

Heimdall and Heimdall and Heimdall.

But who could tell it was Heimdall, that figure on the seashore? The watchman of the gods left his horn Gjall safe in the well of wisdom; he left his golden-maned stallion, behind the stable door; and he strode alone across the flaming three-strand rainbow bridge from Asgard to Midgard.

It was spring and time for sowing. The god walked away from Bifrost over soft green ground and soon he came to the edge of the earth. All day, as the sun fled west from the wolf, he picked his way along the wavy line where the soil meets the deep sea.

At nightfall Heimdall approached a decrepit turfed hut. The evening air was quite still, but the shack was so rickety that it looked as if it might collapse if the eagle-giant Hraesvelg gave one flap of his wings. Heimdall knocked and swung open the roughly hewn door. He had to stoop to get under the lintel and over a pile of sacking on to the shining marl floor. It took the god a moment to adjust to the rank, smoky gloom; his eyes smarted and he retched. Then he made out a trestle table, a bench, more sacking heaped in one corner, a kind of cupboard leaning against a crumbling wall and in the middle of the room the crouched figures of Ai and Edda, Great Grandfather and Great Grandmother, facing each other across the fire.

'Am I welcome?' asked Heimdall.

'What is your name?' said Ai.

'Rig,' said Heimdall.

'You are welcome,' said Edda.

So the god joined Ai and Edda. He spoke honeyed words, as he well knew how, and in no time he had won the best position by the fire. From time to time he peered hopefully into the pot hanging over it. After a while, Edda got to her feet. She shuffled to one corner of the stinking hut, poked about, and dumped a loaf of bread on the table. It was not fully leavened, and was gritted with husks. Then the old woman unhooked the pot of thin broth and put that on the table too. The three of them sat on a rough bench and ate what there was to eat. There was one who was by no means satisfied.

After their meal, Ai and Edda and their guest were ready to lie down and sleep. Again the god spoke honeyed words, as he well knew how, and in no time he had won the best position, in the middle of the bed, with Ai on one side of him, Edda on the other. For three nights the god stayed with Great Grandfather and Great Grandmother. Then he thanked his host and hostess for their hospitality and went on his way.

Every day the two stallions, Arvak Early Waker and Asvid All Swift dragged the chariot of the sun across the sky. And Day himself rode at ease round the world; the shining mane of his stallion lit up earth and heaven. But then Night tightened the reins of her mount and each morning the face of the earth glittered with rime that fell from his bit. The strength of summer weakened and the length of the days shortened. So grim winter showed his fist, full of frost and snow and ice, and wrestling winds.

Soon nine months had passed and Edda gave birth to a son. He was sprinkled with water and his mother swaddled him. He had raven hair, and Ai and Edda called him Thrall.

If Thrall was less handsome than might be desired, he was certainly striking and all of a piece. From the first, his skin was wrinkled; his hands were chapped, his fingers were stubby and his knuckles were knotted. His face was, in a word, ugly. His back was twisted and his feet looked too large for him.

Nevertheless, Thrall was strong, and as the years passed he made good use of his strength. Day in, day out, and all day long, he sweated in the forest, gathering wood. He bound up bundle after bundle of faggots, and carted them home for burning.

When Thrall was a young man, a girl who was his equal in every way came to his hut. She was bow-legged; the soles of her feet were damp and discoloured; her sun-burned arms were peeling; and she had the squashed nose of a boxer. Her name was Thir the Drudge.

Thrall liked the look of Thir, and Thir liked the look of Thrall. In no time the two of them were sitting near the fire side by side,

with eyes only for each other. And in a little more, they had prepared a bed – a bolster and a hairy blanket – and all evening they
sat whispering.

That night was not the last that Thrall and Thir slept together.
They had a cluster of contented children. The names of their sons
were Cattle Man and Coarse, Shouter and Horse Fly, Concubine
Keeper and Stinking, Clot and Gross, the sluggard Drott and Legg-
jaldi whose legs were as thick as tree trunks, Hunch-backed and
Ashen-Face.

These twelve sons shored up the structure and repaired the fabric of
the hut. They spread loads of dung over the land surrounding it.
They took their turn as goatherds and at rounding up the pigs. They
all dug for peat.

Thrall and Thir also had daughters. There were Oaf and Blob Nose,
Dumpy and Hefty-Thighs, Noisy and Servant, Peg of Oak, and Bundle
of Rags; bony Tronubeina had legs as long and skinny as a crane.

These were the offspring of Ai and Edda; and from these children
stem the race of thralls.

Heimdall continued his journey. He took the shortest way to the
next farm, and walked up to the door in the blue hour, just as the
light was fading. The god knocked and entered. In the middle of the
room, a fire flickered, and sitting near it Heimdall saw Afi and Amma, Grandfather and Grandmother.

Afi had a length of wood laid across his lap and was chipping at it
with a knife, shaping a weaver's beam. The knife's blade and the pool
of white shavings at his feet gleamed in the gloom. Afi's hair was
combed and curled over his forehead; he had a trimmed beard.
And his clothes – his leather jacket and breeches – were no less well
cut than his hair.

Amma was unwinding flax from a distaff, spinning thread. She
stretched and she reached, absorbed in her work. She wore a band
round her head and her silver hair was knotted in a bun. She wore a
simple frock and a shawl round her shoulders, secured by a handsome clasp.

'Am I welcome?' asked Heimdall.

'What is your name?' asked Afi.

'Rig,' said Heimdall.

'You are welcome,' said Amma.

So the god joined Afi and Amma. He spoke honeyed words, as he

well knew how, and in no time he had won the best position by the
fire. From time to time he peered hopefully into the pot hanging
over it. After a while, Amma stopped working and got to her feet.
She padded across the room to a stout oak chest and took out a loaf
of rye bread, and a gob of butter, and knives and spoons, and
arranged them on the table. She dipped a large jug into the vat of
beer standing by the door, and then she unhooked the pot of boiled
veal and set that on the table too. Then the three of them sat to eat.

After their meal, Afi and Amma and their guest were ready to lie
down and sleep. The god spoke honeyed words, as he well knew
how, and in no time he had won the best position, in the middle of
the bed, with Afi on one side of him, Amma on the other. For three
nights the god stayed with Grandfather and Grandmother. Then he
thanked his host and hostess for their hospitality and went on his
way.

Every day the two stallions dragged the sun across the sky, and
Day himself rode at ease round the world. But then Night tightened
the reins of her mount, and each morning the face of the earth
glittered with rime that fell from his bit. Summer's strength
weakened, the days shortened. So grim winter showed his fist, full
of frost and snow and ice, and wrestling winds.

Soon nine months had passed and Amma gave birth to a son. He
was sprinkled with water and his mother swaddled him. His cheeks
were ruddy, he had bright eyes, and Afi and Amma called him Karl.
Karl was quick to grow, and he was well built and strong. In time he
learned how to drive oxen with a goad, and how to fasten the share
and coulter to a plough; he found out how to build huts and barns —
how to dig the foundations, and erect a timber frame, and lay the
turf, and pitch a roof; he became a skilful cartwright.

When Karl was a young man, his parents found him a wife as
much to their liking as to his — the fair daughter of a freeman living
near by. On the appointed day, the bridal party brought her in a
wagon to Karl's own farm. She wore a goatskin coat and a veil, and
keys jangled at her waist. So Afi and Amma won a daughter-in-law.
Her name was Snör. Karl and Snör equipped their farm and arranged
things to their liking. They exchanged rings, and laid a colourful
counterpane on their bed. That place became their place; it became
home.

Karl and Snör had a cluster of contented children. They called
their first-born Man and their second Warrior. Their other sons were
Landowner, Thane and Smith who was a master of every craft, Broad

Shoulders, Yeoman and Clipped Beard; Bui and Boddi owned a farm and a barn; Brattskegg had a clipped beard too and like his eldest brother, Segg, was manly. Karl and Snör also had ten daughters. Their eldest they called Snot the Serving Woman. There was Bride and Swan-Neck and Proud, Fair and Womanly; Sprund was as proud as her elder sister; Vif was born to make a good wife, Feima was bashful and Ristil, the youngest, as graceful as any woman.

These were the children of Karl and Snör; and from these children stem the race of peasants.

Heimdall continued his journey. He took the shortest way to a hall near by and, in the late afternoon, strode up to it. Its wide doors faced south, and on one of the posts was a great wooden ring, intricately patterned.

The god knocked and entered. He strode through the long passageway into the hall where the floor was newly strewn with rushes.

In this spacious, gracious room, the god saw Fathir and Mothir, Father and Mother. They sat gazing into one another's eyes; then they touched, just finger ends.

Unaware of their visitor standing and watching, Fathir then busied himself twisting a new bowstring, sharpening arrows, and working at the shape of the carved elm bowshaft itself.

Mothir, meanwhile, sat and considered her slender arms. She smoothed her pleated chemise and drew the sleeves down to her wrists. Her dress had a train. She wore a flowing blue cape, and a charming cap, and on her breast were two oval brooches. This lady was pale-skinned: her brow was fair, her breast gleaming, and her neck was more white than new-fallen snow.

'Am I welcome?' asked Heimdall.

'What is your name?' asked Fathir.

'Rig,' said Heimdall.

'You are welcome,' said Mothir.

So the god joined Fathir and Mothir. He spoke honeyed words, as he well knew how, and in no time he had won the best position by the fire. Mothir lost no time. She took out an embroidered linen cloth and laid it over the table. She brought white loaves of finely ground wheat; bowls worked in silver filigree, full to the brim with cheese and onion and cabbage; well browned pork and horse and lamb; nicely turned partridge and grouse. The pitcher was full not of mead or ale but wine, and the goblets were made of solid silver.

Then the three of them sat to eat. They ate and drank and talked until after dark.

After their meal, Fathir and Mothir and their guest were ready to lie down and sleep. The god spoke honeyed words, as he well knew how, and in no time he had won the best position, in the middle of the bed. Fathir slept on one side of him, Mothir lay on the other. For three nights the god stayed with Fathir and Mothir. Then he thanked his host and hostess for their hospitality and went on his way.

Every day the two stallions dragged the sun across the sky, and Day himself rode at ease round the world. But then Night tightened the reins of her mount, and each morning the face of the earth glittered with rime that fell from his bit. Summer's strength weakened, the days shortened. So grim winter showed his fist, full of frost and snow and ice, and wrestling winds.

Soon nine months had passed and Mothir gave birth to a son. He was sprinkled with water and wrapped in silk. He had fair hair and colour in his cheeks and the look in his glowing eyes was as grim as a snake. Fathir and Mothir called him Jarl. Jarl was quick to master skills. He learned how to hold and hoist a shining shield, and how to wield a lance. Like his father, he twisted bowstrings and shaped bowshafts and loosed quivering arrows. He rode; he unleashed hounds. He learned the art of sword-play, and could swim across sounds.

One day, unannounced, the god walked out of the forest of slender silver birches that stood near the hall. He strode down to the building and found Jarl there, sitting alone.

'Jarl,' he said.

'You are welcome,' said Jarl.

'I've brought you a gift,' said the god. He showed Jarl a bundle of staves carved with signs and coloured red.

Jarl stared at them; he had never seen such things before.

'These are the runes, the magic words.'

Jarl looked at the god, then at the runes, then at the god again.

'Do you know the words against pain of the mind, pain of the heart, pain of the body?'

Jarl shook his head slowly.

'Do you know the words that put water on a fire? Do you know the words that put the sea to sleep?' All that day, the god explained the secret meaning of the runes to Jarl, and Jarl felt excited and ready. He thought all his life had been waiting for this moment.

'I have one more thing to tell you,' said the god, as the light failed. 'What is that?' asked Jarl.

'My son.' The god took Jarl into his arms. 'You are my son,' he said. And he explained how he had visited the hall so long before. 'You are my son; and as I am Rig the King, so will you be Rig the King. Now is the time to win land, to win great age-old halls, and command a host of followers.'

The god looked piercingly at Jarl, his son, then turned on his heel, and walked out of the gleaming hall into the darkness.

Jarl did not need to be told twice. He thought his father's words explained to him what he had always felt but could not name. He was filled with a sense of release and purpose.

At once Jarl left the hall where he had lived since the day of his birth. He rode through a dark forest, and over passes between frosty forbidding crags; and in a place difficult of access, he established his own hall. He gathered a group of loyal retainers.

Jarl shook his spear and brandished his shield; he spurred his horse and dealt death blows with his sword. He brought his followers to battle and stained the soil red. He slew warriors and won land. Before long Jarl owned no less than eighteen halls. He won great wealth and was generous to his retainers. He gave them finger-rings and armbands, both of gold; he gave them precious stones; and he gave them horses lean and fleet of foot. And his retainers called him Rig Jarl, they called him King.

In time Jarl sent messengers over the boggy ground to the hall of the chieftain Hersir. And there, on Jarl's behalf, they asked for the hand of his daughter, Erna. She was fair-haired and long-fingered, and accomplished at whatever she put her mind to.

Hersir was delighted. After Erna had made proper preparation, the messengers escorted her to Jarl's hall, wearing a wedding veil. And she and Jarl lived most happily together.

Jarl and Erna had a cluster of contented children. They called their first-born Bur the Son, and their second Barn the Child; there was Jod the Child and Athal the Offpsring; Arvi was an Heir and Mog another son; there were Nid and Nidjung the Descendants, Svein the Boy, and kinsman Kund; the youngest was Kon, a nobly born son. Soon all the boys learned to play and swim. As they grew older, they tamed beasts, and made circular shields, shaped shafts and shook spears.

But Kon the Young learned from his father the runes, the age-old meanings. In time he was able to blunt a sword blade and put the sea to sleep. He understood the language of the birds, he could quell flames, and quieten cares – the raging mind and aching heart of an unhappy man. He had the strength of eight men.

Kon and Jarl shared their secret understanding of the runes, and Kon was even more subtle and wise than his father. He believed it would be his right, too, to be called Rig the King; and he soon won that right.

One day Kon went riding in the gloomy, dark forest. Now and then he reined in his mount and loosed an arrow at a luckless bird. Other birds he lured from their perches, and listened to them.

A crow sat on a branch over Kon's head. 'Kon,' it croaked, 'why do you spend your time seducing birds to talk to you? You would do better to set out on your stallion and show daring in battle.'

Kon listened carefully to the crow's counsel. The darkness seemed to fall back from the clearing where he stood, and to wait in the wings.

'Who have halls more noble than yours?' continued the crow. 'Who have won riches greater than yours – gold and jewels and precious ornaments?'

Kon did not answer; he clenched his fists.

'Who are more skilled than you at steering their ships over the reach of the sea and the stinging saltspray?'

Still Kon did not answer.

'Dan and Damp, Dan and Damp, Dan and Damp,' sang the crow. It looked sideways at Kon. 'They know what it means to temper their weapons with the blood of enemies . . .'

The manuscript breaks off here and so the myth is incomplete Its purpose was probably to establish the divine descent of Danish kings.

THE MEAD OF POETRY

WHEN the gods made a truce, and settled terms for a lasting peace, every single god and goddess spat into a great jar. This put the seal on their friendship, and because they were anxious that no one should forget it, even for one moment, the gods fashioned a man, out of the spittle.

His name was Kvasir. He was so steeped in all matters and mysteries of the nine worlds since fire and ice first met in Ginnungagap that no god nor man nor giant nor dwarf ever regretted putting him a question or asking his opinion. And wherever Kvasir went, news of his coming went before him. When he reached some remote farm or hamlet, sewing and salting and scything and sword-play were laid aside; even children stopped chattering and listened to his words.

What was his secret? It was as much in his manner as in his mine of understanding. Questions of fact he answered with simple facts. But to ask Kvasir for his opinion – What shall I say? What do you think? What shall I do? – did not always mean getting a direct answer. Sitting back in his ill-fitting clothes, as often as not with his eyes closed, he would listen to recitals of problems and sorrows with a kind, grave, blank face. He took in and set everything in a wider frame. He never intruded or insisted; rather, he suggested. Often enough he answered a question with another question. He made gods and men, giants and dwarfs feel that they had been helped to answer their own questions.

The stories of Kvasir's wisdom soon reached the ears of a most unpleasant pair of brothers, the dwarfs Fjalar and Galar. Their interest soon turned to envy and their envy to energy, for they could not admire anything without wanting it for themselves. They asked Kvasir to feast with them and a large gathering of dwarfs in their cave under the earth and, as was his custom, Kvasir accepted. The table was a long slab of uneven rock, the floor was grit and the wall-hangings were dripping stalactites; the talk was chiefly of profit and loss and petty revenge; the food, however, and the tableware, all made of hammered gold, were rather more pleasing.

After the feast, Fjalar and Galar asked Kvasir for a word in private. Kvasir followed them into a gloomy chamber, and that was a mistake. The two dwarfs had knives hidden in their sleeves, and at once they buried them in the wise man's chest. His blood spurted out of his body and Fjalar and Galar caught it all in two large jars and a cauldron. Kvasir's heart stopped pumping and his drained white body lay still on the ground.

When, after a while, the Aesir sent a messenger to ask after Kvasir, the two dwarfs sent back word that he had unfortunately choked on his own learning, because there was no one in the nine worlds well-informed enough to compare and compete with him.

But Fjalar and Galar were delighted with what they had done. They poured honey into the jars and cauldron filled with Kvasir's blood, and with ladles stirred the mixture. The blood and honey formed a sublime mead: whoever drank it became a poet or a wise man. The dwarfs kept this mead to themselves. No one else tasted it; no one even heard about it.

One day the dwarf brothers entertained two gruesome guests, the giant Gilling and his wife. It was not long before they began to quarrel and Fjalar and Galar became more and more spiteful and full of hate. They suggested that Gilling might enjoy the sea breeze, and each taking an oar, rowed far out into the ocean surrounding Midgard. Then the dwarfs rammed their boat into a slimy, half-submerged rock. Gilling was alarmed and gripped one gunwale. His alarm was well-founded; the boat foundered and capsized. Gilling was unable to swim and that was the end of Gilling! The two dwarfs cheerfully righted their craft and rowed back home, singing.

Fjalar and Galar described what had happened to Gilling's wife.

'An accident,' said Fjalar.

'If only he had been able to swim,' Galar said sadly.

Gilling's wife wept and wept and, sitting in their cave, the two dwarfs did not like the feel of the tepid water washing round their ankles. 'I've an idea,' whispered Fjalar to his brother. 'Find a millstone, and go and wait above the entrance to the cave.'

Galar got up and went outside and Fjalar asked the giantess: 'Would it help if you looked out to sea? I could show you the place where he drowned.'

Gilling's wife stood up, sobbing, and Fjalar stepped aside for her as befits a host. And when the giantess stepped out into the daylight, Galar dropped the millstone on to her head.

'I was sick of her wailing,' said Fjalar.

When Gilling and his wife did not return to Jotunheim, their son Suttung set out in search for them. He looked at the dwarfs' dismal faces and listened to their lengthy tales and then he seized both of them by the scruffs of their necks.

Holding one in each hand, a pair of danglers, he angrily waded a mile out to sea, until it was too deep even for him. Then Suttung dumped Fjalar and Galar on a skerry, a sopping rock standing just clear of the water. 'It's much too far for you to swim,' he said. 'Much too far. So when the tide rises . . .'

Fjalar looked at Galar and both brothers grimaced.

'We've a suggestion,' said Fjalar.

'Since it has come to this,' said Galar, 'we're willing to offer you our greatest treasure.'

Then Fjalar described their mead, both its origin and power, with a wealth of words.

'Give us our lives,' said Galar, 'and we'll give it to you.'

'Agreed,' said Suttung.

So Suttung took the two dwarfs back to their cave and, since they clearly had no choice, they handed over Kvasir's blood. The giant stumped back to Jotunheim, carrying a jar in each hand and the cauldron tucked under his arm. He took the precious liquid straight to the mountain Hnitbjorg where he lived. Suttung hewed a new chamber out of the rock at the heart of the mountain and hid the three crocks in it. And he told his daughter Gunnlod that she had one duty: 'Guard this mead by day and guard it by night.'

Unlike the dwarf brothers, Suttung was boastful about his treasure. So it was not long before the gods learned about the divine mead,

and heard how it had fallen into Suttung's unholy hands. Odin himself elected to go to Jotunheim and bring the mead back to Asgard.
The One-eyed God disguised himself as a giant of a man, and called
himself Bolverk, worker of evil. He crossed the river that divided
Asgard and Jotunheim and strode across a desert of shifting grey grit
where nothing, not even a grassblade, could take root. Bolverk came
to a curtain of mountains. He hurried over a snowy pass and at last
walked down into a narrow green valley.

Nine thralls were working in a sloping field, men from Midgard
with a taste for adventure and handsome reward. They were scything
the succulent grass with long, slow sweeps, and seemed very weary.

'Who is your master?' Bolverk asked one thrall who had stopped
work entirely.

'Baugi,' said one thrall.

'Baugi?'

'Suttung's brother,' the thrall said, 'the giant who guards Kvasir's
blood.'

'Shall I sharpen your scythe?' asked Bolverk affably.

The thrall was rather quick to agree to this, and when Bolverk
drew a whetstone from his belt and began to put a new edge on the
scythe, the other thralls crowded round in the hope he would hone
their scythes too. Bolverk obliged, and the thralls all said that their
scythes had never been quite as sharp before; they complained that
the giant Baugi was too hard a taskmaster; they pointed to acres of
grass, still uncut, that lay before them; coming to the point, the
thralls asked whether they could buy Bolverk's whetstone.

'I might think about selling it,' said Bolverk, 'but only to one
man; and only to the one – if there is such a man here – who will
feast me tonight in the manner to which I'm accustomed.'

The air was filled with shouts of agreement. 'Yes,' the thralls
shouted. 'Yes . . . Me . . . I will . . . Here . . . All right . . . I'm your
man . . . Done . . . Agreed . . . Your hand on it!'

Bolverk looked at them with his one eye. He smiled grimly. Then
he threw the whetstone into the air. In the sun it glinted, it looked
like silver.

The thralls gasped. They raised their scythes and ran, all of them
eager to be under the whetstone when it fell. It seemed to hang in the
air, so high had Bolverk tossed it. The thralls jostled, they stepped
backwards, they suddenly swung round; and in the end, in their
confusion, they all slit one another's throats. The nine of them lay in
the long grass they had just cut.

Still smiling grimly, Bolverk caught the whetstone, tucked it into his belt, and walked back the way he had come.

The sun dawdled, and so did Allfather. Not until nearly midnight did he come down from the mountains again, and make his way to Baugi's farm. He said his name was Bolverk and explained that he had been walking all day. Then he asked Baugi if he could give him some kind of a meal and let him stay overnight in one of the huge barns near to the farmhouse.

'A fine time to ask,' said Baugi abruptly.

Bolverk looked pained and asked Baugi what was wrong.

'All my farmhands have been killed. That's what is wrong! Baugi banged his fist on a trestle table, a blow so powerful it would have flattened a man's head. 'All nine of them. And how can I hope to find any more at this time of year?'

'I've an idea,' said Bolverk. 'You can see I'm strong. Very strong. I can take on the work of nine men.'

Baugi looked Bolverk up and down, and smiled in disbelief, thinking Bolverk was a hollow boaster. 'And if I agreed, what wages would you ask?'

'Only this,' said Bolverk. 'One drink of Suttung's mead.'

Baugi sniffed and shook his head.

'I may be strong,' said Bolverk. 'But to be a poet: that's the finest calling.'

'That mead is nothing to do with me,' said Baugi. 'My brother has it in his safe-keeping; and no one except Gunnlod has ever seen a drop of it. That's how things are.'

'Well,' said Bolverk. 'Those are my terms.'

Baugi shrugged his shoulders and so Bolverk got up to leave.

'I can talk to Suttung,' said Baugi. He had little love for his brother; but he felt sure that, in any case, Bolverk would never be strong enough to keep his part of the bargain. 'Work for me this summer, and I'll tell my brother how you helped me out. That's the best I can do.'

'How far can I trust you?' said Bolverk.

'You'll see,' said Baugi.

For as long as the long days, Bolverk worked for Baugi. As the sun climbed out of the east, Bolverk walked to the green fields still thick with the honey-dew that fell every night from the branches of Yggdrasill. All day he worked under the bright skull of the sky. He worked while the sun hurried west until it seemed to hang, blood red, on the western skyline. Baugi was amazed that Bolverk was as good as his boast, and seemed to need so little rest; he thought now that Bolverk must be more than merely human.

At the end of the summer, Bolverk asked Baugi for his wages. They went together to find Suttung at Hnitbjorg, and Baugi told his brother how Bolverk had helped him and asked for one drink of the divine mead.

'Never,' said Suttung. 'Not a drop!'

'Well,' said Bolverk as soon as he was alone with Baugi, 'I hope you're not going to accept Suttung's answer. I've worked for you all summer.'

'I've kept my promise,' Baugi said.

'Why should he have it all for himself?' said Bolverk. 'Don't you fancy a mouthful, Baugi? Since your brother won't part with the mead willingly, let us see if we can trick him out of it.'

'Impossible,' said Baugi. 'Do you know where it is hidden?' He was rather nervous of Suttung; but he was also rather nervous of Bolverk. Bolverk pulled an auger out of his belt, and told the giant that with it he might be able to drill a hole through the mountain. 'This is the least you can do in return for my work.'

Baugi took the auger and pressed the shank against the sheer rock face of the mountain Hnitbjorg; with both hands he turned the handle. He wondered how to get rid of the troublesome farmhand as he wound and wound and the auger sank into the mountain.

'There!' exclaimed the giant. 'Right through!' He withdrew the drill and wiped his brow.

Bolverk peered with his one eye into the dark passage left by the auger. Then he filled his lungs and blew fiercely into it. A shower of rock chippings blew back into his face, and Bolverk knew that Baugi had not, after all, cored the mountain. 'Were you trying to cheat me?' he said.

The giant said nothing. He drilled further into the mountain, silently vowing to dispose of Bolverk as soon as he could.

When Baugi withdrew the auger once more and Bolverk blew down the hole a second time, all the loose chippings were carried forward on the tide of air. Then Bolverk knew that the giant had bored right into the room at the heart of Hnitbjorg. At once he turned himself into a snake and shrithed into the hole.

Baugi stabbed at Bolverk with the point of the auger but he was not quick enough; the snake was already half-way down the passage on his way to Gunnlod and the divine mead. As soon as he reached the stronghold, Bolverk changed himself back into a giant of a man –

one-eyed but handsome – and stood in front of Suttung's daughter.

Gunnlod was sitting on a stool of solid gold. And at the sight of Bolverk, Suttung's stern warning that she should guard the mead flew right out of her head. She was not sorry to have company. She sat and listened to Bolverk's beguiling words and songs; she wrapped her arms around him; for three days they talked and laughed and for three nights they slept together. In the silent cave under Hnitbjorg, the heartless father of the gods made love to the spellbound daughter of Suttung. Then Gunnlod was drunk with passion and ready to give Bolverk whatever he desired. He asked for three draughts of Kvasir's blood and Gunnlod took his hand and led him to the mead. With his first draught Bolverk emptied the cauldron, with his second draught one jar, with his third draught the other jar. The father of the gods held all the divine mead in his mouth.

Then Odin turned himself into an eagle, flapped down the passage out of Hnitbjorg, and headed for Asgard. Suttung saw him and at once murmured the magic words known only to those who have drunk divine mead. Gods and giants and men and dwarfs saw a dark sight – one eagle pursuing another towards the kingdom of Asgard.

The Aesir quickly brought out jars and bowls, and laid them side by side so that they covered the whole courtyard just inside the great wall of Asgard. Anxiously they watched as Suttung came closer and closer to Odin.

The distant rustle became a whirr, and the whirr a terrible flapping and beating of wings. There was only a wingspan between the two birds. Then the eagle Odin dived in over the wall and spat the mead into the crocks assembled beneath him.

In his haste to escape Suttung, Odin could not help letting some mead spill outside the wall, but it was so little that the gods were not bothered about it. They said that anyone who wanted it could have it; and that became the poetaster's portion.

Suttung shrieked and wheeled away and shrieked again. He had lost through cunning what he had won through force, and there was nothing he could do.

And the gods? They had lost wise Kvasir, witness to the friendship of the gods. But because of the cunning of Allfather, they had won back his blood. Once more Odin drank some of the precious mead. And from time to time he offered a draught to one of the Aesir or to a man or two in Midgard; he offered them the gift of poetry.

LOKI'S CHILDREN
AND THE BINDING OF FENRIR

NOT content with his faithful wife Sigyn, Loki sometimes took off for Jotunheim; the Trickster hurried east and spent days and nights on end with the giantess Angrboda. Loki and Angrboda had three monstrous offspring. The eldest was the wolf Fenrir; the second was Jormungand, greatest of serpents; and the third was a daughter called Hel. Even in a crowd of a thousand women, Hel's looks were quite likely to single her out: her face and neck and shoulders and breasts and arms and back, they were all pink; but from her hips down, every inch of Hel's skin looked decayed and greenish-black. Her expression was always the same: gloomy and grim. When the gods heard that Loki had fathered these children, they were filled with alarm. They discussed what to do about them at the Well of Urd and the three Norns gave them little encouragement.

'Their mother is evil,' said Fate.

'But their father is worse,' Being said.

'Expect nothing from them but the worst,' said Necessity. 'Expect them to harm you and endanger you. They will be in at the kill.'

And so the gods agreed that Loki's children must be captured. At Odin's behest, a group of gods crossed into Jotunheim by night; they burst into Angrboda's hall and gagged and bound her before she had even rubbed her eyes; then they kidnapped her children and carried them back to Asgard.

Odin was in no doubt as to what should be done with the serpent. He picked up Jormungand and hurled him into the ocean surrounding Midgard, the world of men. He hurtled through the air, smashed through the iron face of the water and sank to the sea bottom. There he lived and there he grew. Jormungand, the Midgard Serpent grew so thick and so long that he encircled the whole world and bit his own tail.

Odin was just as sure what to do about the serpent's sister. He took one look at Hel and hurled her out of Asgard, too. He threw her into the mist and darkness of Niflheim, the world beneath the worlds. And as she fell she heard Odin's decree that she should look after the dead, all those in the nine worlds who died of illness or old age, the condition being that she should share out whatever food she had with whoever came to her.

Hel made herself at home: beyond the sheer rock, Drop to Destruction, she built huge walls around her estate. Her hall, home of the dead, lay within it, behind a massive pair of gates. Hel's manservant and maidservant moved about so slowly that it was not easy to tell whether they were moving at all; her plate was called Hunger, and her knife Famine. Her bed was Sick Bed, and the bed-hangings Glimmering Misfortune.

Odin thought it would be best if the gods themselves kept an eye on Fenrir. He seemed no different to any other wolf, and all the gods agreed that there would be no harm in letting him roam around the green and golden fields of Asgard. Even so, of all the gods only Tyr, son of Odin, was brave enough to face Fenrir alone, and give him great joints – flesh and gristle and bone – to keep him quiet.

The gods were not slow to change their minds about Fenrir when they saw him growing larger day by day. And when the Norns renewed their warnings, and said that the wolf would cause Odin's death, their alarm became far greater. They agreed that since they could not kill the wolf there and then and stain the sanctuary of Asgard with his evil blood, they must catch and fetter him. Then the gods made a powerful chain of iron links and they called it Laeding. Several of them went up to Fenrir, showed him the chain, and asked: 'Are you as strong as this?'

The wolf inspected Laeding. 'It's certainly strong, but I'm certainly stronger,' was all he had to say as he let the gods wind the chain round his neck and body and legs, until there was only a small length left for them to hold on to.

'Finished?' snarled the wolf. He planted his massive paws well apart, filled his lungs with air, then flexed every muscle in his body. Laeding's links at once sprang apart, and the gods sprang back alarmed.

The gods lost no time in making another chain. This was called Dromi, and it was twice as strong as Laeding. The links were larger than those of the largest anchor chain; no men could have even moved them. 'If you can break this chain,' the gods told Fenrir, 'you will be known for your strength throughout the nine worlds.'

Fenrir looked at Dromi. He thought it looked immensely strong, but then he thought that he too had grown even stronger since he had snapped Laeding. 'No one wins fame without taking a risk,' was all he had to say as the gods wound the vast chain round his neck and body and legs.

'Finished?' snarled the wolf. He shook so that there was a terrible clinking and clanking and grating; he rolled over and arched his back and banged the chain against the ground; he tightened his muscles until they were as hard as the iron links of Dromi; he stood up again and dug his paws into the earth and strained and strained – and all at once, Dromi snapped. It shattered into hundreds of separate links; the shrapnel flew in every direction. After this, the gods were frightened; they thought they might fail to fetter Fenrir.

'But if anyone can make a fetter that will not break,' Odin said, 'the dwarfs can.' And he sent off bright Skirnir, Freyr's messenger, to the world of dark elves. Skirnir went down under Midgard through gloomy, dark, twilit grottoes. There he found Nar and Nain and Niping and Dain and Bifur and Bafur and Bombor and Nori and hundreds of others, each one as horrible as the next, and promised them gold and more gold if they could make a fetter for Fenrir. In the gloom the dwarfs' eyes gleamed like glow-worms; they whispered and schemed and set to work. They made a fetter as smooth and supple as a silk ribbon, and they called it Gleipnir.

When he returned to Asgard, Skirnir was thanked by all the gods for going on this mission. 'But what is it made of?' asked Odin, fingering the fetter.

'Six things,' said Skirnir. 'The sound a cat makes when it moves; a woman's beard; the roots of a mountain; the sinews of a bear; the breath of a fish; and a bird's spittle.'

The gods were both astonished and sceptical of Gleipnir's power.

'If you doubt it, as I doubted it,' said Skirnir, 'remember the cunning of the dwarfs. After all, have you ever thought why a cat makes no noise when it moves, and why a woman has no beard? You can never prove that a mountain has no roots, but many things that seem not to exist are simply in the dwarfs' safekeeping.'

Then a large group of gods approached Fenrir for the third time. They invited him to go out with them to an island in the middle of a lake.

There the gods produced the silken ribbon Gleipnir. They showed it to Fenrir and challenged him to test his strength against it.

'It's a little stronger than it seems,' said one.

'It's as well-woven as the words of a good poem,' said another. 'But you, Fenrir, you'll be able to break it.'

The wolf looked at Gleipnir. 'This ribbon is so slender,' he said, 'that I'd win no fame for snapping it.' He eyed Gleipnir again. 'If, on the other hand, cunning and magic have gone into its making, then slender as it looks, you can keep it for yourselves. I'm not having it wound round my legs.'

'Before this,' said one god, 'you've prised apart massive iron fetters. You'll have no bother with this band.'

'And if by any chance you're unable to break it,' said another, 'we'll set you free again, you can trust us.'

Fenrir showed his teeth and the gods did not like the look of them. 'If you're able to fetter me,' he snarled, 'it will be a long time before I can hope for any help from you.' Fenrir prowled right round the group of gods. 'I don't want to be bound with that ribbon. But neither do I want to be accused of cowardice. So while the others bind me, let one of you put his hand in my mouth as a token of your good faith.'

Tyr looked one by one at all the gods in that company. All the gods there looked at each other and said nothing, wondering what to do. Then Tyr slowly lifted his right arm and put his hand in Fenrir's mouth.

At once the other gods wound Gleipnir round and round the wolf's neck and body and legs, until it was all used up. Fenrir began to struggle against it. He tried to kick and shrug and shake and jerk and roll; but the more he strained the tighter Gleipnir became. Then Fenrir snarled and clamped his teeth; Tyr, bravest of the gods, twisted and cried out, unable and able to bear such pain. The other gods laughed, they knew that Fenrir was bound at last. They all laughed except Tyr: he lost his hand.

The gods fixed a large chain to the end of the silken ribbon. They passed the end of this chain through the hole in a huge boulder, looped it back, and secured it to itself.

The gods drove the boulder a mile down into the earth. Then they found a vast rock and dropped that on top of the boulder to fasten it. Fenrir shook and wrestled. He grated his teeth and gulped and opened his blood-stained jaws immensely wide. Then one of the gods drew his sword. He drove the point hard into the roof of Fenrir's mouth and rammed the hilt against his lower jaw. The wolf was gagged. Fenrir was gagged and Fenrir was bound. His howls were terrible, and slaver streamed from his jaws. It ran from the middle of the island into the lake and was called the River of Expectation.

And just as the Midgard Serpent waits at the bottom of the ocean, coiled round the world; just as Hel waits in Niflheim, surrounded by corpses and swirling death-mist; so, gagged and bound on the island, Fenrir lies and waits for Ragnarok.

THE THEFT OF
IDUN'S APPLES

VERY early one summer morning, Odin, Loki and Honir crossed into Midgard, happy in one another's company, and intent upon exploring some part of the earth not already known to them.

In the pale blue, almost pale green light that gives an edge to everything, the three friends crossed a desolate reach of grit, patrolled only by the winds. Before men in Midgard had stirred and woken, the gods were striding over scrubby, undulating ground. Then they tramped round a great mass of spiky, dead, dark rock, and headed for the summit of a conical mountain.

All day they trekked and talked and, in the evening, they followed the course of a rapid, milky river from a glacier down into a valley – a jigsaw of fields, yellow and brown and green.

Odin, Loki and Honir had not brought any food with them and were beginning to feel very uneasy about it when they had the luck to come across a herd of oxen. While Loki sized them up, chose one and killed it, Odin and Honir gathered fallen branches from a grove of stunted oaks and made a fire. Then they cut up the ox into huge pieces and put the pieces into the heart of the fire.

The smell ravished the gods; they could barely wait to eat. As soon as they thought the joints were roasted, they scattered the fire and pulled the meat out of the flames.

'It's not ready,' said Odin, surprised. 'We must be so hungry that a little time seemed long to us.'

Loki and Honir raked up the brands and put the meat back into the fire again.

Suddenly a chill wind channelled down the valley. Although the sun still loped across the western sky with the wolf at its heels, all the heat had drained out of the summer sky. The three gods wrapped their cloaks around them and sat and waited.

'Do you think it's ready?' asked Honir. 'What do you think? Shall I find out?'

'One of these days, you'll choke on your own uncertainty,' Loki said, leaping to his feet and scattering the fire for a second time. 'It must be cooked by now.'

Odin took a piece out of the flames. 'It's still not ready,' he said. 'And it ought to be.'

'There's nothing wrong with this fire,' Honir said.

'And yet our dinner is as raw as it was to begin with,' said Loki, looking at the meat and grimacing.

'Well,' said Odin, 'something is working against it.'

'Something sitting up here,' said a voice from above them.

The three gods at once looked up into the leafy branches of the oak tree above the fire. They looked and they saw an eagle sitting there, and it wasn't a small one.

'Let me eat my fill,' said the eagle to the three upturned faces, 'and your ox will be cooked.'

The gods conferred and were of one mind. 'Since we too want to eat tonight,' Odin told the eagle, 'we agree. There is nothing else we can do.'

Then the eagle screeched. It flapped its immense wings, swooped down from the tree and settled over the fire. At once it greedily snatched up both the shoulders and both parts of the rump as well. Then it eyed the gods and, crouching at the root of the oak, began to eat. Loki was so angry that he raised his staff and rammed it into the bird's body. The eagle was thrown off balance and dropped the meat. It screeched again and took to the air. One end of the staff was firmly lodged in the eagle's back; and, to his alarm, Loki found that he was unable to let go of the other. He pulled and twisted and yelled to no purpose. His hands were stuck to the staff.

The eagle flew at great speed and it took care to fly close enough to the ground to make sure that Loki did not have a smooth ride. The Trickster was dragged across the floor of Midgard. His knees and ankles banged into boulders; his legs and feet were scratched by gorse bushes and thorns until they were bleeding.

'Mercy!' shouted Loki.

The eagle took no notice. It dragged Loki on his backside across a glacier until he was all but skinned.

'Mercy!' yelled Loki again. He thought his outstretched arms were going to be wrenched from their sockets.

'Only,' said the eagle, rising to give Loki a little respite, 'only if you will swear . . .'

'What?' shouted Loki. 'Anything! Mercy!'

'Only if you will swear to bring the goddess Idun and her apples out of Asgard.'

Loki closed his eyes and pressed his lips together and said nothing. He knew now that the eagle could only be one of the giants, in disguise. The eagle swooped again and Loki could hardly bear the pain as his knee-caps and shins and ankles and toes cracked against rocks and boulders and scree.

'Mercy!' implored Loki. 'I promise you. I swear it.'

'Seven days hence,' said the eagle. 'Lead Idun over the rainbow bridge when the sun is half-way between east and west.'

'I promise,' called Loki.

The Trickster found that his hands were at once set free and he fell to the stony ground. Very slowly he picked himself up and looked at his wounds. Then, in the gathering darkness, he began to limp back towards his companions.

Seven days passed and Loki found Idun wandering through the sloping field above her hall. She was singing softly to herself, and was quite carefree; the sun caressed her. Childlike she moved, untroubled by the world's troubles around her, petty squabbles, suffering, savage wars, and, always, time passing. Her basket of golden apples was looped over one arm.

'Idun!' called Loki.

The goddess paused and turned.

'I've come at once. You can't imagine; I could scarcely believe it myself.'

'Speak more simply,' said Idun.

'Deep in the forest just beyond Bifrost, I came across a tree quite unlike the others. Unlike any tree I've seen in the nine worlds. It stands in a glade and it glows with a soft light.'

Idun opened her grey eyes wide, and Loki went on to describe his find so carefully that anyone less trusting would have known it came straight out of his head.

'Idun, it bears golden apples,' he said, jabbing with his forefinger at one of the apples in the basket. 'The same as yours. And perhaps, like yours, they contain unending youth. We should take them at once for the gods.'

Idun smiled and nodded in agreement.

'Bring your own apples. We must compare them,' said Loki, and he led the way over the sunlit field and out of Asgard. They hurried past the watchman Heimdall's hall and then Loki took Idun by the hand and walked with her over Bifrost. The flames danced around their feet and they were unharmed.

The eagle was waiting. As soon as Idun set foot in Midgard, it rose from a thicket. It beat its dark wings, swooped on the goddess, and snatched her up. It carried her and her apples straight over the sea to Jotunheim – for as Loki had suspected, the eagle was none other than a giant. It was Thiazi.

Thiazi lifted the goddess to his storm-home, Thrymheim, high in the mountains. 'Here you'll stay,' he gloated. 'Without you, without your apples, the gods will age, and I will remain young for ever.'

*   *   *

When they missed Idun, the gods at once grew extremely anxious. They knew that without her magic apples, they would wither and grow old. And, indeed, they soon began to crumple inside their clothes and to seem smaller than they were before. Their skin hung over their bone-houses, bunched or puffy or wrinkled, or stretched so tight that it looked as though the bone would break through. The eyes of one became bloodshot and the eyes of another misty; one god's hands began to tremble, one lost all his hair, and one could not control his bowels. Their joints creaked and ached and they felt utterly limb-weary. The gods felt the spring in their step and the strength in their bodies ebbing from them hour by hour.

Then the minds of the gods lost their skip and started to soften. One became outspoken about the shortcomings of the others and one began to ramble like an idiot, but most of the gods grew quiet and did not trouble to say many things they would have said before. And they were all obsessed by the same concern with time, the same fear. When they did speak, they repeated themselves; or they began sentences and did not complete them. The summer sunlight shone on Asgard, flocculent clouds drifted overhead, and the minds of the gods wandered even as they worried about their old age.

Odin knew he must rally his own strength and summon the gods to council. Everyone in Asgard made his way to the great hall Gladsheim, a dismal straggling procession under the sun. Of all the gods and goddesses and their servants, only Idun and Loki were missing.

Allfather looked at the great gathering of stooping, shuffling, mumbling figures. 'We must find Idun,' he called. 'You see how it is without her, without her apples. And it will grow worse. Who was the last to see her?'

'I saw Loki lead her over Bifrost,' said Heimdall's servant.

There was a deep silence in Gladsheim. No one doubted then that Loki was the cause of what had happened to them.

'There is only one thing to do,' said Odin. 'We must capture Loki.'

Weary as they were, the gods searched for the Trickster; they looked in every hall and outbuilding, and in every copse and corner of Asgard; they knew their lives depended on it. At last they found him asleep in Idun's own field, and they seized and bound him before he could do anything about it.

Loki was brought to Odin's hall, protesting, and there Odin at once charged him with leading Idun out of Asgard. 'Bring her back,'

said Allfather. 'Your choice is easy to explain and easy to understand. Bring Idun and her apples back. Otherwise we'll put you to
death.'

'It is true,' said Loki, 'that I walked out of Asgard with Idun. But
then I had no choice.' Loki told them how the eagle that had carried
him off when he was trekking with Odin and Honir was none other
than the giant Thiazi. 'And I had to agree to those threats to escape
with my life,' said Loki.

'Did you have to fulfil them?' asked Odin.

Loki's eyes gleamed, red and green.

'Since you consort with eagles,' said Odin, 'we'll draw a blood-
eagle on your back.'

'No,' said Loki, and he shrank before Odin's savage eye.

'And your rib-cage will spring apart.'

'No,' said Loki, cowering.

'Like wings,' said Odin and his teeth were clenched.

'I will find Idun and her apples,' said Loki. 'If Freyja will lend me
her falcon skin, I'll fly at once into Jotunheim. I swear it.'

Then Odin shook and released Loki, and Freyja, beautiful Freyja,
her face like a pouch now and her hair falling out, went directly to
her hall with him. She pulled down the falcon skin hanging over
one of the beams.

'You're not quite so beautiful now you're bald,' said Loki.

Freyja said nothing. Her body shook. She wept tears of gold and
handed Loki the falcon skin.

*   *   *

Thrymheim perched on the top of a precipitous sgurr and seemed actually to grow out of the dark rock. The winds whirled round it, and found their way through the walls into the cold, draughty rooms. When Loki reached it in the early evening, he was fortunate enough to find the giant Thiazi was not at home. He had gone off fishing, and his daughter Skadi had gone with him.

Loki discovered Idun in a smoky room, huddled over a fire. She turned to him and at once the Trickster extended his falcon wings; he murmured the runes, the magic words, and turned Idun into a nut. Then he picked her up between his claws and flew off as fast as he could.

In a little time, Thiazi and his daughter returned from the day's fishing. When the giant found that Idun was no longer there, he roared and hurled his pails to the ground. He knew there was no way in which the goddess could have escaped from Thrymheim without help.

Then Thiazi donned his eagle skin for a third time and set off across the mountains and the high lifeless wilderness. The distance from Thrymheim to Asgard was immense and the eagle was stronger than the falcon. As Loki drew closer to Asgard, so Thiazi drew closer to Loki.

When he sat in his high seat, looking over the nine worlds, nothing escaped Odin: no movement of man or giant or elf or dwarf, bird in the air or animal on earth or fish in the water. What other gods could not see at all, Allfather fixed and followed with his single eye. Now he saw Loki flying at great speed towards Asgard and the eagle Thiazi chasing him. At once he ordered all the gods and goddesses and their servants, worn out and short-winded as they were, to hurry out of Asgard with bundles of plane shavings, all the wood that the servants of the gods had readied to kindle fires in their great halls. 'Pile them up against the walls,' said Odin. 'Loki is coming.'

The still summer air began to hum, as if an unseen storm were near and about to burst upon them. It began to throb and then the gods and goddesses saw the falcon, and the huge eagle close behind it. From a great height the falcon dived down over the walls of Asgard, still holding the nut between its claws. 'Light the shavings!' cried Odin. 'The shavings!'

The flames leaped up, almost unseen in the bright sunlight. The eagle was so close behind the falcon that he could not stop himself; he flew straight through the flames; his wings caught fire. Thiazi blundered on into Asgard, and fell to the ground in torment. Then the gods stumbled back through the gates into their citadel and quickly killed him there.

Loki threw off Freyja's falcon skin. He looked at the grey, aged, anxious ones pressing around him, and scornfully laughed in their faces. Then the Trickster bent over his trophy; he cradled it between his hands and softly spoke the runes.

Idun stood there, young and supple and smiling. She moved innocent among the ailing gods. She offered them apples.

THE MARRIAGE OF
NJORD AND SKADI

B
EYOND the girdle of flint-grey water and the loveless lava
flows, beyond the burning blue crevasses, lay Thrymheim,
the storm-home of Skadi and her father Thiazi. It was a
wonder that the hall withstood the charges of the wind and the
batteries of hail.

Thiazi was not there; he had gone in pursuit of his prisoner Idun,
the goddess who had escaped him. Skadi waited for them to return
and, as the sun slipped over the horizon, the sky in the west seemed
to catch fire and blazed.

The white night dallied and yielded; another dawdling day passed
and still Thiazi and his captive did not come back. Then Skadi was
alarmed and thought the gods must have ambushed him; even as
she waited, she knew in her heart she would never see her father
again.

Skadi's pale eyes gleamed. She grew cold with anger, then icy with
fury. She swore vengeance on his murderers.

Skadi walked from chill room to chill room in Thyrmheim. She
donned a coat of mail and a helmet and chose the finest of her
father's weapons: a sword engraved with magic serpentine pattern-
ing, a spear with a shaft of ash, a circular shield covered with hide

and inlaid with birds of prey – gleaming gold eyes and gaping red beaks. Then she set out for Asgard.

Now that Idun walked among them again and the giant Thiazi was dead, now that they had recovered the apples of youth, the Aesir were carefree once more. They were aware of the clement sun as if they had never felt it on their backs before; they listened to each note of each birdcall, and watched every glassblade growing. They felt at peace with themselves again, and at peace with each other.

When Heimdall saw Skadi nearing the walls of Asgard and raised the alarm, the gods had no wish to see more blood spilt, or to prolong the feud. Some of them gathered and met the giantess and asked her, 'Will you take gold for your father's death?'

'What good would that be?' asked Skadi. 'Have you never heard of my father's wealth? When his father died, he and his brother came into a gold hoard. They measured it out in mouthfuls, so as to share it fairly. And whatever belonged to my father now belongs to me. No, I will not take gold.'

'What will you take?' asked the gods.

'A husband,' said Skadi, and she looked long at Balder, fairest, most gentle and wise of the gods. 'I'll settle for a husband and a bellyful of laughter.'

Then the gods conferred and agreed that Skadi could choose a husband from amongst them as payment. They did, however, make one condition. 'You must choose him by his feet,' said Odin. 'Until you've chosen, that is all you'll be able to see of him.'

Skadi was not unwilling and Odin arranged for all the gods to gather in a courtyard so that the giantess could make her choice. Shielding her eyes from all but the gods' feet, Skadi lost no time but at once chose the most shapely pair of feet, believing that they would naturally belong to Balder, the most handsome of the gods.

'A good choice,' said Odin.

Skadi quickly looked up and gazed into the friendly, knowing eyes not of Balder but of the lord of seafarers and sea harvests, the god Njord. His skin was weathered and he had the clear gaze of one who has spent long at sea; he even smelt of salt.

Skadi was startled. She stepped back, and her icy look killed Njord's smile. 'I thought . . .' she began.

'Think carefully,' said Njord. 'Remember the words you speak now are the beginning of a marriage.'

'I've been tricked,' said Skadi bitterly.

'You might have chosen Loki,' replied Njord unperturbed.

'So you have your husband then,' said Odin. 'A fair reward for your father's death; many would say, indeed, the better of the bargain.'

'You've forgotten the laughter,' said Skadi.

'That's easily put right,' said Odin.

Skadi shook her head. 'Since my father died, I've brimmed with anger or been drained by fatigue. I'll never laugh again.'

'Where's the Trickster?' asked Odin.

Loki stepped forward rather less jauntily than usual. He wondered whether Skadi knew that he had not only helped her father to steal the apples, but helped the gods to recover them too, and so brought about her father's death.

'Can you make this lady laugh?' said Odin. 'If anyone can you can.'

'Not I, sir . . .' stammered the Sly God, as if he were some peasant standing before the High One. 'Not before I've told you what happened, sir . . .' Loki produced a long leather thong from behind his back. 'It was like this. I was going to market and I wanted to take that goat there along with me.' Loki winked at Skadi. 'You know how goats are, don't you, lady? They have ideas of their own.'

Loki stumbled across the courtyard where all the gods and Skadi were assembled, and tied one end of the thong to the goat's beard. 'Both my hands were full, lady. I was carrying produce to the market. So I tied this goat to a hose . . .'

'A hose?' said Skadi.

'Lady,' said Loki, 'my hose!' And he looped the thong over his long hose. The goat moved a little further off to nibble at new grass, and the thong linking them tightened.

'Early in the morning it was, lady,' said Loki. 'Ah! Very early. The goatsuckers were still singing . . .' The Trickster cupped his hands to his mouth, closed his eyes, and made a magical soft whirring sound. 'Rrrr . . . rrrrrrr . . . rrrrrr . . . OWK!' squawked Loki, as the goat suddenly yanked the thong.

'Owk!' squawked the goat as Loki pulled back. It was a tug of war. And when the goat gave way, it gave way so completely, bounding towards Loki, that he fell backwards into Skadi's arms.

And Skadi laughed; despite herself she laughed, and for a while she forgave Loki everything because of her laughter.

'Playing the goat,' said Loki, panting.

'Enough,' said Allfather. 'I've a mind to please Skadi further.' Then Odin took two liquid marbles from his gown and Skadi recognised her father's eyes.

'But look!' cried Odin.

He hurled the balls into heaven. 'Two stars,' he said. 'Your father will look down on you and on us all, for as long as the world lasts.'

Then Njord asked Skadi to go with him to his hall, the shipyard Noatun, but Skadi said she would only live with Njord in her old home, Thrymheim. 'Since neither of us is going to get his way entirely,' said Njord, 'we had better agree to take turns: nine nights in one place, then nine nights in the other.'

Then Njord and Skadi left the courtyard and the kingdom of Asgard, and made their way to Jotunhiem. They climbed over rock and scree, and through sheets of snow too bright for the eye when the sun shone on them, a dreary uniform wasteland when clouds masked the sun. And the higher they climbed into a frozen world as still as death itself, the happier Skadi became. In Thryheim, she gave herself to Njord. After nine nights, however, Njord admitted that he had no love for the icy mountains. 'And,' he said, 'I think the howling of wolves sounds ugly compared to the hooping of swans.'

Then Njord and Skadi came back to Asgard and passed nine nights at Noatun, and Skadi's dislike of the fertile, rocking sea was no less great than Njord's dislike of the barren mountains. 'I cannot even sleep here,' she said. 'There's too much noise in the shipyard, and too much noise from the harbour – boats putting out, boats coming in, the unloading of fish. And the mewing gulls disturb me, flying in at dawn from deep waters.'

It was not long then before Njord and Skadi decided that the gap between their taste was so great that, although they were married, they must live apart. Njord stayed at Noatun and Skadi returned to Thrymheim.

The giantess covered great distances on her skis; her quiver was always at her side and she hunted and shot wild animals. The ski goddess, that crouched dark shape sweeping across the desolate snowscapes, took injury and death wherever she went. She had been touched by the god of plenty; she had yielded a little; and then she froze again.

THE TREASURES
OF THE GODS

SOMEHOW the Shape-Changer got into the locked bedroom of
Sif, Thor's wife. Smiling to himself, he pulled out a curved
knife and moved to her bedside. Thor's wife was breathing
deeply, evenly, dead to worldly sorrows. Then Loki raised his knife.
With quick deft strokes he lopped off Sif's head of shining hair – her
hair which as she moved rippled and gleamed and changed from
gold to gold like swaying corn. Sif murmured but she did not wake;
the hair left on her cropped head stuck up like stubble.

Loki scooped up the skeins. He dropped Sif's sheen hair to the
floor, a soft glowing mass. The Trickster looked at it and grinned;
then he left Sif's bedroom.

'A joke,' protested Loki, dangling a foot off the ground.

'What kind of a joke?' shouted Thor, not loosening his grip for
one moment.

'Only a joke,' whined the Trickster.

All morning Sif had sobbed and sobbed. She knew and Thor knew that only Loki would have shorn her hair. 'Well, what are you going to do about it?' demanded Thor.

'I'll replace it,' yelped Loki. 'I'll get help from the dwarfs. I promise to replace it.'

'Or else,' said Thor, and he dumped Loki on the ground.

Loki raised both hands and cautiously explored the top of his head.

'Or else,' Thor said, 'I'll smash every bone in your body.'

Loki straightened his clothes and smoothed his hair and then suddenly he winked at Thor. He hurried out of Asgard, over Bifrost, and down into the land of the dark elves. He picked his way through a chain of chilly potholes, and he skirted dark and shining pools, until he reached a great cave, the home of the sons of Ivaldi.

The sly god explained to the two dwarfs the reasons for his journey, without finding he need describe just how Sif had lost her hair. 'Only you dwarfs are skilled enough smiths,' he said, 'and only the sons of Ivaldi could spin gold as fine as Sif's hair and imbue it with such magic that it will grow on her head.'

'What will we get out of this?' was all that the sons of Ivaldi wanted to know.

'The thanks of Sif and Thor and the friendship of the gods,' said Loki. 'That counts for a great deal. And, above that, I give you my oath that I'll repay you in full measure when you have need of me.'

The dwarfs could see that although Loki offered nothing but promises, they were likely to get the better of the bargain, since the most they could lose was a little effort and a few ounces of gold. They piled wood on to the furnace in the corner of their cave, and while one dwarf worked the bellows, the other began to hammer and spin the gold. Loki watched and marvelled, and his eyes flickered red and green in the firelight.

The sons of Ivaldi made a long wave of fine golden strands and, as they worked, they murmured spells over them. The hair hung over Loki's outstretched arm like a single shining sheet and yet a breath of air was enough to ruffle it.

'To waste this blaze is to no one's advantage,' said one of the dwarfs.

'We can please the gods at no further expense,' said the other.

So the sons of Ivaldi set to work again and, before the furnace had begun to lose any of its heat, they fashioned a marvellous ship for Freyr called Skidbladnir and forged for Odin a spear called Gungnir, as strong as it was slender. Then the two dwarfs gave Loki the ship and the spear and explained their magic power. As usual Loki was at no loss for words – his mouth was full of air, thanks and compliments and promises to hurry back with news of what the gods thought of such gifts.

On his way back through the dismal underground caverns, Loki had an idea. He did not head straight for the welcoming light of Midgard, but turned down a long aisle studded with rock pillars and, carrying his three treasures, walked into the hall of the brothers Brokk and Eitri.

The two dwarfs stood up to greet Loki. But when they saw the skein of hair and the ship and the spear, they ignored him entirely. Their hearts quickened and their fingertips tingled. Loki let them take the treasures out of his hands and turn them over and over.

'Have you ever seen such work?' exclaimed Loki. 'Such perfect craftsmanship?'

'Yes,' said Brokk.

'Whose?' asked Loki.

'My own,' said Eitri bluntly.

'Well then,' said Loki slowly, as if the thought were just forming in his mind, 'you think you could make treasures as fine as these?'

'Not as fine . . .' Brokk said.

'Finer,' said Eitri.

'No,' said Loki craftily. 'Surely not. I'll stake my head on it. Brokk, I'll stake my head that your brother can't forge treasures the like of these.'

Brokk and Eitri were very eager to take up this challenge. It occurred to them that if they were as good as their boast, not only would they be rid of the schemer Loki but the treasures made by the sons of Ivaldi would be theirs for the taking.

Leaving Loki with a horn full of mead and with orders only to wait, Eitri and Brokk stumped across their hall and through an arch into the rocky alcove that was their smithy. At once Brokk began to pile wood on to the furnace while Eitri hammered and rolled a length of gold wire and cut it into hundreds of short pieces. Then Eitri laid a pigskin on the roaring fire and said to Brokk, 'Pump the bellows now. Whatever happens, keep pumping until I pull this treasure out of the forge.'

A little while after Eitri had walked out of the smithy, a fly alighted on Brokk's leathery hand. It stung him. Brokk glanced down but did not pause; he kept pumping the bellows, and when Eitri returned he pulled Gullinbursti out of the forge, a boar with bristles of gold.

Now Eitri picked a great block of unflawed gold. He heated the metal until it was glowing and malleable. Then he hammered it into shape and put it back into the furnace. 'Pump the bellows now,' said Eitri. Whatever happens, keep pumping until I pull this treasure out of the forge.'

A little while after Eitri had left the smithy, the same fly returned and settled on Brokk's neck. It stung him twice as sharply as before. Brokk winced and flinched but he did not pause; he kept pumping the bellows, and when Eitri returned he took Draupnir out of the forge, an arm-ring of solid gold.

Now Eitri humped a great hunk of iron across the smithy and into the furnace. He heated it and hammered it. He struck at it and shaped it, he reshaped it, he tapped and tapped at it. His body ached, he streamed with sweat and, when he was ready, his head and heart were both banging with his own efforts. 'Pump the bellows now,' said Eitri. 'It will all be wrecked if you stop pumping.'

Very soon after Eitri had walked wearily out of the smithy, and looked around for their visitor, the fly buzzed through the arch into the alcove. This time it settled between Brokk's eyes, and at once it stung him on both eyelids. The dwarf was blinded with blood. He could not see what he was doing. For a moment he took a hand off the bellows, so that they caught their breath, to brush the fly off his forehead and the blood out of his eyes. Then the Shape Changer, Loki, for the fly was none other, returned to his waiting place and his horn of mead.

At this moment Eitri hurried back into the smithy. 'What has happened?' he shouted. He peered into the furnace. 'So nearly,' he said. He peered into the flames again and his glittering grey eyes did not even reflect them. 'So very nearly spoiled.' Then Eitri pulled from the forge an iron hammer, massive and finely forged, but rather short in the handle. He called it Mjollnir. Eitri and Brokk stared at it; they stared at each other; they slowly nodded.

'Take this hammer and this ring and this boar,' said Eitri. 'Tell the gods the mysteries of these treasures. Go with Loki to Asgard and claim that schemer's head.'

Brokk and Eitri walked out of the alcove and found the Trickster, the Shape Changer, waiting for them, smiling. He cast an eye over their three treasures. 'Ready?' he said.

*   *   *

Loki and Brokk made their way slowly across the shining fields of
Asgard, laden with their treasures. Word of their coming ran ahead
of them, and they were met in Gladsheim by all the gods, sitting in
their high places. Loki at once told of his visit to the world of the
dwarfs; he boasted that he had been able to exploit the dwarfs' envy
and greed to secure no less than six gifts for the gods.

'Talk while you can,' said Brokk. 'Soon you'll have no tongue.'

It was agreed that Odin and Thor and Freyr should decide whether
Eitri or the sons of Ivaldi were the finer smiths, and Loki began to
display his treasures.

'This spear,' he said, 'is for you, Odin. It is Gungnir. It differs from
other spears in this way: it never misses its mark.' The Father of
Battle took the spear and raised it and looked around the hall. Nobody could withstand his terrible gaze. 'You may want to use it,'
Loki said, 'to stir up warfare in the world of men.'

Then Loki turned to Freyr. 'This vessel is for you, Freyr. It is
Skidbladnir. As you can see, it's large enough to hold all of the gods,
fully armed. As soon as you can hoist its sail, a breeze will spring up
and fill it, and urge the boat forward. But when you have no need of
it, you can take it apart.' Loki swiftly dismasted and dismantled the
boat until the pieces were together no larger than a piece of cloth.
'You can fold it up like this,' said Loki, 'and put in in your purse!'

'My third gift,' said the schemer, 'I owe to you, Sif.' He showed
the skein of flowing golden hair to the goddess. 'As soon as you lift
this to your head, it will take root and grow. You'll be no less
beautiful than you were before.'

Thor's wife took the hair from Loki. She fingered it, she turned it
over and over, then she slowly raised it to her head. There was a
shout of joy in Gladsheim.

Now Brokk produced his gifts. 'This gold arm-ring is for you,
Odin,' he said. 'It is Draupnir. There is a little more to it than it
seems. Eight rings of its own weight will drop from it on every
ninth night.'

Then Brokk turned to Freyr. 'This boar is for you. He is Gullinbursti. He can charge over earth, air and sea alike, and no horse can
keep up with him. And no matter where he goes, running through
the night or plunging into the gloom under all the worlds, he'll
always be surrounded by brilliant light. He carries it himself because
his bristles shine in the dark.'

'My third treasure,' said Brokk, 'is for you, Thor. This is the hammer Mjollnir. You can use it against anything, and use it with all

your strength. Nothing can ever break it.' The Storm God eagerly grasped the hammer and listened. 'Even if you hurl it, you'll never lose it. No matter how far you fling it, it will always return to your hand. And should you need to hide it, you can make it small enough to tuck inside your shirt.' All the gods stared at Mjollnir, astounded, and knew what powerful magic must have gone into its making. 'It has only one small flaw,' added Brokk, 'not that it matters. Its handle is rather short.'

Odin and Thor and Freyr wasted no time in giving their answer. All three were of one mind that, wondrous though all the treasures were, the hammer Mjollnir was the most valuable because it alone could guard the gods against the giants.

'You, Brokk,' said Odin, 'have won the wager.'

'Loki's head,' shrieked Brokk.

'Wait!' cried Loki. 'What would you do with my head? I'll give you its weight in gold instead.'

'There's no future in that,' said Brokk. 'And no future for you.'

The gods in Gladsheim laughed to see the Trickster cornered.

'Well,' said Loki slowly, 'well . . . catch me then!' He darted through the doors of the hall and made off as fast as he could. By the time Brokk had made a move to stop him, the Sky Traveller was already well on his way, wearing his shoes with which he could fly over land and water. The gods in Gladsheim laughed all the louder.

'If you had any honour, you'd help me,' shrieked the dwarf. 'Thor, help me!'

Thor was in no mood to see Brokk humiliated. He leaped up from his high seat and stormed out of Gladsheim. The gods and Brokk waited, and after a while Thor returned, dragging Loki after him.

'Not so fast!' said Loki, raising a hand, as Brokk started towards him. 'It's true you have a claim on my head. But of course you can't have any part of my neck.'

The gods grinned and nodded, and Brokk saw that Loki had got the better of him.

'In that case,' said Brokk, 'since your head is mine, at least I'll stop your sweet talk. I'll sew your lips together.'

Loki shrugged his shoulders. 'Nothing but fine words!' he said.

Brokk unwound a thong from round his waist and tried to skewer Loki's lips with his knife. That was no good. Sharp as the point was, the dwarf could not even draw a drop of blood.

'I could certainly do with my brother's awl,' said Brokk. No sooner had he spoken than Eitri's awl lay at his feet. Brokk picked it up, and it proved sharp enough to pierce Loki's lips. The dwarf drew the leather thong through the holes and sewed up the Trickster's mouth.

Loki ran out of Gladsheim. He ripped the thong put through the holes, and yelped at the pain of it. Then for some while the Trickster stood listening to the hum inside the hall – the hive of happiness. He began to dream of revenge, and slowly his lips twisted into a smile.

SKIRNIR'S JOURNEY

FREYR had no business to be in Odin's hall, Valaskjalf. And he had no right at all to sit in his high seat and look out over all the worlds. That was the right only of Odin and his wife Frigg. Freyr narrowed his eyes and looked north into Jotunheim. What did he see? A large handsome hall belonging to the giant Gymir. And what did he see next? A woman coming out of this hall. Her name was Gerd – she was Gymir's daughter. She seemed to be made of light, or clothed in sparkling light. When she raised her arms to close the hall doors, the dome of the sky and the sea surrounding the earth at once grew brighter. Because of her, all the worlds were hidden in a flash of brilliant icy light.

Freyr looked and longed. The more he looked, the more he was unable not to look. His eyes burned like fireballs; his only desire was to win Gerd. Freyr gazed at her until she had crossed a court-yard into her own hall. The worlds grew shadowy and the god lowered his eyes; then he left Valaskjalf and crept out of the hall.

Freyr paid for presuming to sit in Odin's high seat. He ached with an endless sad longing. He spoke to no one and wanted no one to speak to him. He could not sleep. He did not want to eat.

He did not want to drink. He could neither escape his fierce desire, nor see how to satisfy it.

Njord, Freyr's father, became concerned about his son. He called for Freyr's servant, shining Skirnir, and told him: 'Go and ask my son what has upset him. Why is he so angry, or else so sad, that he will not even share his feelings and set them free?'

'I will ask him that,' said Skirnir, 'but I won't like the answer.'

Skirnir approached Freyr and said to him, 'First of the Gods, why must you stay here in your hall, day in and day out, without food or drink or sleep? Why do you shun company?'

'What good would it do?' said Freyr. 'No amount of talk can help, nothing can blunt this anguish. And what if the elf-beams do shine every day? My mind is full of gloom.'

'There is no grief so great you cannot tell it to me,' said Skirnir. 'We were children together. We've always trusted one another.'

Then Freyr unlocked his word-hoard. He told Skirnir how he had seen Gerd from Odin's high seat, and how she brightened the nine worlds with her radiance, and how he longed for her. 'No man,' he said, 'has ever loved a woman as I love her. And no god would ever agree to our union.'

Skirnir listened and nodded.

'Go!' said Freyr. 'Whether her father likes it or not, bring her to me here, and I'll give you great rewards.'

Skirnir smiled. 'Give me the horse that follows its nose through the dark, and will not bridle at magic, flickering flames. And give me the sword that will fight against giants of its own accord.'

Then Freyr handed over two of his greatest treasures. He lived to regret that: at Ragnarok, a sword to ward off the fire-demon Surt would have been handy.

Skirnir mounted and made off at once. As he galloped out of Freyr's courtyard, his horse's hooves struck fire from the paving stones. In the early evening, Skirnir was ferried across the river into Jotunheim, and then night fell. 'Can you feel this darkness pressing against us?' said Skirnir to the horse, and they galloped across lifeless flatland. 'Now we must head for the fells, where the frost giants live. You and I share the same fate. We'll either get home again quickly, or we'll fall into the hands of some dreadful troll.'

Skirnir rode through the night, and during the night he and his mount climbed a mountain pass and came to a curtain of fire. Freyr's horse did not even break its pace and galloped straight through the searing magic flames. At daybreak Skirnir, the Shining

One, came down into a saucer of land covered with sour grey grass. It was a loveless kind of place, surrounded by desolate hills that welled like breasts and were pocked by outcrops of rock. In the middle of this depression stood Gymir's hall and, next to it, his daughter's hall, guarded by a fence. A pair of hounds were chained to the gateposts, and they were not pleasant.

Skirnir looked around and saw a single herdsman sitting way up on the hillside. He turned away from the halls and rode up to him. 'Nothing escapes your eye,' Skirnir said, 'sitting here on this hill. Tell me, how can I muzzle those hounds and enter Gerd's hall?'

The herdsman looked at Skirnir and said stonily. 'Are you doomed to die? Or are you dead already? There's no way in which you can talk to Gymir's daughter; not this year or next year; never!'

Skirnir could see that the herdsman did not mean to help him. He wheeled away without more ado and, as he galloped down the slope again, called out over his shoulder, 'Fearlessness is better than a faint heart for any man who puts his nose out of doors. The length of my life and the day of my death were fated long ago.'

In her hall, fair Gerd heard the coming and going, barking and shouting, and asked her servant, 'What is all that noise that echoes round the walls? The ground shakes; the hall itself shudders.'

'A man outside the fence. He's dismounting now. And now he has set his horse to graze.'

'Welcome him, then,' said Gerd coldly. 'My heart says this visitor is my brother's murderer. Nevertheless tell him a horn of mead awaits him in this hall.'

So Skirnir passed unharmed between the disappointed hounds and walked into the hall; it was colder in there than he would have wished.

Dressed entirely in white, Gerd came forward to welcome him. 'Are you one of the elves? Or one of the gods? How were you able to pass through the flickering flames to these halls?'

'I'm no elf,' said Skirnir, 'and I'm no god, though it's true that I've come through the fire curtain.' He looked at Gerd and dipped his hands into the pockets of his cloak. 'These,' he said, 'these are eleven of the apples of youth. They're yours, Gerd. I'll give them all to you if you'll promise yourself to Freyr and call him your darling dear.'

'Never,' said Gerd icily. 'No one is going to buy my love with golden apples and promises of youth. And however long we live, Freyr and I will never share one roof.'

Skirnir reached into the pocket of his cloak again. 'I've brought you this arm-ring,' he said. 'It is Draupnir. Eight rings of its own weight drop from it on every ninth night.'

'Be that as it may, I have no wish for it,' said Gerd, and her voice chilled Skirnir to the marrow. 'There's wealth enough in Gymir's hall.'

Skirnir continued to smile. 'You see this honed and gleaming sword here in my hand? I'm going to hack off your head unless you do as I ask.'

'Force will get Freyr nowhere,' said Gerd. Her cold eyes glittered. 'Neither Freyr nor anybody else. But if my father Gymir finds you here, I'm sure he'll be glad to flex his muscles.'

Skirnir was undaunted. 'Look again at this honed and gleaming sword. The old giant will fall to his knees before this blade; your father is doomed to die.' Then Skirnir laid down Freyr's sword and raised his own staff. Gerd gazed at it spellbound. 'I will touch you, Gerd, with this magic staff. I will teach you and tame you. You must make your way to the place where you'll never meet and never talk to any man again. You will sit on the eagle's hill at the end of heaven and stare down at Hel's gates. And although you must eat, all food will seem as vile to you as the sallow snake seems to men.

'You'll become a sight to make our blood run cold. The frost giant Hrimnir will gape at you. You'll become better known than the watchman of the gods as you peer out, bleakly, from your windy penthouse.

'Rage and longing, tears and torment will rack you. However you twist and turn, you'll not escape your fate: a troubled heart, a double portion of misery.

'Here in Jotunheim, spiteful spirits will pick at you and prick you every day, and every day you will crawl to the halls of frost giants – crawl for no purpose, and crawl without even hope.

'While others are glad, you will grieve, your body will shake with sobs. You'll live always amongst three-headed giants and never once sleep with a husband. May lust grip you! May despair sap you! Be like thistle tossed into the hayloft and trampled underfoot!

'I went to the dark wood, the dripping forest, to find a magic branch. I found this staff. The greatest of the gods, Odin, is enraged with you. Freyr will waste no love on you. Gerd, worst of women, you have unleashed the wrath of all the gods.

'Frost giants, listen! Rock giants, listen! Sons of Suttung, listen! And hear me, gods in Asgard! I forbid this woman to meet with any man. I forbid this woman joy of any man.

'Hrimgrimnir, pale and unearthly in his shroud of frost, is the giant who will enjoy you in the gloom near Hel's gates. Under the roots of Yggdrasill, foul corpses will press on you horns full of piss. However great your thirst, that is the best drink there will be for you. That is my curse!

'Gerd, I have inscribed a charm for you, sealed with three runes: longing and raving and lust. But what I have written, I can erase, if I have good reason.'

As she listened to Skirnir's spells, Gerd began to tremble terribly. At length she raised her eyes, slowly, and gazed at her guest.

'Skirnir,' she said, 'you are welcome here. Drink from this frost-cup filled with mead for you.' Now her eyes no longer glittered like broken ice; they were filled with tears. 'I never believed,' she said, 'that I should swear to love one of the gods.'

Skirnir lowered his staff and took the frost-cup. 'Before I ride home, I must know everything. When will you meet Freyr, son of Njord?'

'There is a forest, Barri, that we both know well. It is beautiful there, and peaceful. And there Gerd will give herself to Freyr, son of Njord, nine nights hence.'

Then Skirnir bowed. He took his leave of Gerd and walked out of her chilly hall. He called his horse to him, remounted and rode swiftly back to Asgard before it was morning.

Sleepless, Freyr heard him coming. He stood outside his hall, impatient and anxious.

Skirnir smiled and, taking his time, dismounted.

'Skirnir! Before you unsaddle, before you go a foot further, tell me! Were you successful? Have you brought ecstasy or anguish out of Jotunheim?'

The god and his servant stood in a shaft of soft orange light near the entrance to Freyr's hall. Skirnir gathered his cloak around him and looked at Freyr. 'There is a forest, Barri, that we both know well. It is beautiful there, and peaceful. And there Gerd will give herself to the son of Njord nine nights hence.'

'One night is long,' cried Freyr, 'and two nights are longer. How can I bear three? How can I . . .' He raised his arms and threw back his head and closed his eyes. 'Often enough I've thought a whole month shorter than half one such night, charged with this desire.'

THOR RETRIEVES
HIS HAMMER

W HEN Thor awoke and reached out to grasp his hammer, it was not there. The Hurler leaped up. He tousled and tangled his red beard; his hair bristled as he searched for Mjollnir.

'Listen, Loki!' said Thor. 'No god in Asgard has seen my hammer; no man in Midgard has seen my hammer: it has been stolen.'

Then Thor and Loki hurried to Freyja's hall. They well knew that if the hammer were not found, it would not be long before the giants stormed Asgard's walls and brought the bright halls of the gods crashing to the earth.

'Will you lend me your falcon skin,' asked Loki, 'so that I can search for Thor's hammer?'

'If it were fashioned of silver,' cried Freyja, 'you could use it. I would lend it even if it were spun out of gold.'

Then Loki donned the falcon skin. The feather dress whirred as he climbed into the moving air, and left the world of the gods behind him. He flew until Asgard became no more than a bright haze away to the west; he flew as fast as he could until at last he reached the world of the giants.

Thrym, king of the frost giants, felt at ease with the world. He had unteased and combed his horses' manes; he was sitting on a green mound, plaiting gold thread, making collars and leashes for his horrible hounds.

When the Sky Traveller saw Thrym, he swooped down beside him.

'How are things with the gods?' said Thrym. 'How are things with the elves? And what brings you to Jotunheim alone?'

'Things are bad for the gods,' said Loki. 'Things are bad for the elves. Have you stolen Thor's hammer?'

Thrym laughed, and the sound was like the chuckle of broken ice. 'I've hidden Thor's hammer eight miles deep in the earth. No one is going to touch it unless he brings Freyja here to be my bride.'

Loki grimaced and the sound of Thrym's freezing laughter followed him as he climbed again into the sky. The feather dress whirred. He left the world of the giants behind him and flew as fast as he could until at last he returned to the world of the gods.

Thor was waiting in the courtyard of his hall and at once asked the Sky Traveller, 'What's in your head and what's in your mouth? Truth or trouble?' The Thunder God's eyes blazed and it was clear that he would brook no nonsense. 'Stand here and tell me the truth at once. A sitting man forgets his story as often as not, and a man who lies down first lies again afterwards.'

'I bring trouble and I bring truth,' said the Sly One, the corners of his crooked mouth curling. 'Thrym, king of the frost giants, has your hammer. And no one is going to touch it unless he brings Freyja to be his bride.'

Then Thor and Loki hurried to Freyja's hall for a second time and found Freyja there.

'Well, my beautiful!' said Loki, narrowing his eyes. 'Put on your bridal veil.'

'What?' retorted Freyja.

'We two must hurry,' answered Loki, grinning. 'You and I are going to Jotunheim. Thrym, king of the frost giants, has taken a fancy to you.'

Freyja was so angry that the walls of her hall shuddered. The gold-studded benches started from the floor. Then Freyja snorted; her face became fiery; her breasts rose and fell; her neck muscles bulged. Then suddenly the marvellous Necklace of the Brisings burst apart – the links snapped and a shower of precious stones rolled around the hall. 'How would it look if I went with you to Jotunheim?' demanded Freyja.

Loki raised his eyebrows; Thor sniffed and shifted from foot to foot.

'Go away!' said Freyja. 'Both of you.'

Then every god headed for Gladsheim, the hall with the silver thatch, to sit in solemn council and discuss how to recover Mjollnir. The goddesses joined them there. The watchman Heimdall had left his hall and the trembling rainbow bridge. He said, 'Let us swaddle Thor . . .' He paused and looked around '. . . swaddle Thor in the bridal veil!'

There was a moment of silence and then a howl of laughter from the assembled gods and goddesses.

Heimdall waited until the uproar had died down and then he went on: 'Let us repair the Necklace of the Brisings and secure it round his . . . his pretty neck.'

Once again Gladsheim erupted and Thor looked across at Heimdall with profound distaste. But Heimdall was unabashed. 'He must be decked as befits any bride. A bunch of jingling keys must hang from his waist. And he must wear a becoming dress – as long a dress as possible! We musn't forget to pin well-wrought brooches on her . . . on his breast.'

This care for detail delighted the gods and goddesses; and they also saw the force of Heimdall's argument.

'And he'll need a charming cap,' concluded Heimdall in a sing-song voice, 'a charming cap to crown it all.'

Thor scowled, 'You'll all mock me and call me unmanly if I put on a bridal veil,' he said.

Then Loki called out insolently, 'Silence, Thor! There's no argument. Giants will live in Asgard if we don't retrieve your hammer.'

So the gods and goddesses swaddled Thor in a bridal veil. They repaired the Necklace of the Brisings and clasped it round his neck. They hung a bunch of jingling keys from his waist, and he wore a becoming dress down to his knees; they pinned well-wrought brooches on his breast, and they crowned it all with a charming cap.

'I'll be your maidservant,' warbled Loki. 'We two will hurry to Jotunheim.'

The Thunderer's goats were rounded up and driven to his hall. There they were harnessed, and impatiently bucked and wrestled with their halters.

Gaping fissures opened in the fells, flames scorched the earth, and Thor, the son of Odin, galloped with Loki to Jotunheim.

'She will come!' shouted Thrym in a frenzy. 'She's coming! Stir your great stumps! Spread straw on the benches! They're bringing Freyja to be my bride.'

Thrym strode up and down his chilly hall, checking the arrangements. Then he sat on a bench and said to himself: 'I've cattle in my stables with horns of gold; I've jet black oxen – beasts to gladden the heart of any man. I've piles of precious stones, and mounds of silver and gold.' Thrym's thoughts evaporated in the cold air, and he sighed, 'I've had everything I wanted – everything except Freyja.'

When the travellers from Asgard arrived at Thrym's hall in the early evening, they were welcomed with great ceremony. The same giant servants who had spread straw on the benches now served up a fine supply of good food and drink.

Thrym ushered Thor, in his bridal veil, to the feasting table. With all the courtesy he could command, he pointed out the fine fare drawn from earth, sea and air alike in her honour. Then he led his intended bride to one high seat and himself sat in the other. Loki promptly ensconced himself next to Thor on the other side.

Thor felt hungry. He devoured an entire ox, and followed that with eight salmon. Then he scooped up and scoffed all the delicacies set apart for the women. And to round things off, he downed three horns of mead.

Thrym watched this feat with growing surprise and anticipation. 'Who has ever seen a bride with such hunger, such thirst?' he exclaimed. 'I've never met a woman who took such huge mouthfuls or who drank so much mead.'

The subtle bridesmaid sitting at Thor's side took it upon herself to answer Thrym. 'Freyja has not eaten for these past eight nights, so wild was her desire for her wedding night.'

Thrym leaned forward and peered under the veil; he could not wait to kiss her. The giant king was so startled that he leaped back the whole length of the hall. 'Her eyes!' he shouted. 'Why are Freyja's eyes so fearsome? They're like burning coals.'

The subtle bridesmaid sitting at Thor's side took it upon herself to answer Thrym. 'Freyja has not slept for these past eight nights, so wild was her desire for her wedding night.'

Now Thrym's luckless sister walked up to the bride and bridesmaid, and she was not half-hearted about asking for a dowry. 'If you want my love,' she said, 'and my loyalty, give me the rings of red gold on your fingers.'

'Bring forward the hammer!' called the king of the giants. 'Bring forward the hammer, Mjollnir, to hallow the bride. And may the goddess Var hear our marriage oath and give us her blessing.'

The Thunder God's unsparing heart sang and danced when he saw his hammer. As soon as it was placed between his knees, he snatched it up in his mighty grasp, swept off his veil and stood revealed as the god, Thor, the Hurler.

Thrym leapt up from his high seat and his companions leapt up from their benches.

Thor's eyes were as red as his beard. He glared at the company of giants and growled. Then he raised his hammer, took one massive step towards Thrym, and crushed his skull. Thor showed no mercy: he felled all the other giants and giant women at that bridal feast. The hall floor was strewn with a host of bodies. Thrym's luckless sister had dared ask for gold rings but she received ringing iron – Thor's hammer on her head.

And so Thor, the Son of Odin, won back his hammer.

THOR'S EXPEDITION
TO UTGARD

THOR said summer was the open season and he announced his plan of making a journey east to Utgard and flexing himself against the giants. 'However few they are,' he said. 'they are too many.'

'In Utgard,' said Loki, 'you'll need sharp wits.'

'Sharp wits,' repeated Thor seriously.

'And yours are as blunt as your hammer,' said Loki, winking at Thor. 'Why not take me?'

Thor ignored the insult and accepted the offer. 'Evil creature: good companion,' he said.

Loki's eyes gleamed, now brown, now green, now indigo. His scarred lips parted a little and twisted into a wolfish smile.

'Tomorrow, then,' said Thor.

Very early in the morning, before the sky turned blue and before a cock crowed, Thor had his goats harnessed to his chariot. Thor and Loki took their seats and Thor grasped the reins of twined silver. The chariot rattled across the plains of Asgard, still soaked with dew, and Thor looked lovingly at the halls of the sleeping gods and goddesses – towering hulks, all of them silent and dreamlike in the ashen light.

They passed through the great gate and headed for Midgard, the home of men. All day the Charioteer and the Trickster rode and talked, at ease with each other and the world. And early in the evening they came to a lonely farm, the only building for miles around. It was low-slung and almost as green as the fields surrounding it; the turfed roof seemed to grow out of the ground.

'A very poor place,' said Loki.

'What they cannot provide I will,' said Thor. He pulled up his goats and climbed out of the chariot.

The farmer Egil and his wife and their children, Thialfi and Roskva, stepped out of their farmhouse and then started to tremble when they recognised their visitors.

'What we want,' said Loki, 'is food and shelter for the night.'

'We'll gladly give you shelter,' said Egil.

'And we can offer you the little food we have,' said the wife. 'Vegetables, potage; there's no meat.'

'Not even a chicken?' said Loki, looking around him.

The farmer slowly shook his head.

'We'll use my goats then,' said Thor. Without ado he slaughtered both animals, and skinned them; then he cut them into joints and jammed them into the wife's large cauldron.

Egil and his wife, their long-legged son and fair daughter felt almost sick with hunger at the thought of such a feast; they kept looking at the meat to see whether it was cooked. Thor spread the skins of his two goats some way from the fire. 'As you eat,' he said, 'throw the bones on to the skins.'

They all sat down together under the stars. 'Mind what I said,' Thor enjoined them. 'Be careful with the bones and throw them all on to the skins.' Then they all began to eat.

The farmer's son, Thialfi, had gone hungry for so long that he could not bear the thought of wasting good marrow. While Thor was talking to his father, he grasped one thigh bone and quickly split it with his knife and sucked the rich juice from it. Then he tossed it on to the heap of bones covering the skins.

After they had eaten Thor and Loki and the farmer's family were ready to sleep. And they all slept soundly after such a fine meal. Thor was the first up; just before daybreak he rose and dressed and went out of the farmhouse. Then he took his hammer, Mjollnir, raised it over the goatskins and hallowed them.

At once the goats stood up, fully fleshed and bleating. But as they began to move about, Thor noticed that one goat had a lame hind leg. He hurried back into the farmhouse. 'Who?' he shouted, and the walls of the farm trembled so much that they nearly collapsed.

Egil and his wife were shocked out of their sleep and sat straight up in their bed. 'Who disobeyed me?' roared Thor. 'I can see a thighbone has been broken.'

Thor's eyebrows beetled and the farmer and his wife and Thialfi and Roskva cowered. His eyes burned like orange flames and the family thought their days in Midgard had come to an end. Then, when the Thunderer grasped his hammer, so that his knuckles turned white, the farmer's wife and Roskva screamed in terror. 'Mercy!' pleaded Thialfi, screwing up his eyes. 'Mercy! Mercy!' And Egil begged, 'My land, my farm, everything I own. Take them. Take everything I own and spare our lives.'

If Thor was sometimes furiously angry, he was never angry for long. When he saw how the whole poor family were panic-stricken, the blood stopped racing round his body. 'I'll take Thialfi and Roskva to be my servants,' he said roughly. 'And that's an end to the matter.'

Now Thor and Loki were ready to resume their journey. Thor gave the goats and the chariot into Egil's care. He said he would collect them on his way back, and told Thialfi and Roskva to follow him to Utgard.

They walked for a long time until at last they came to the girdle of water dividing the world of men from Jotunheim. They stared at the fretful grey water and the mountains beyond – squat tubs and barrels of unfriendly land suppressed by leaden sky.

'That can wait until morning,' said Thor.

Then they busied themselves with putting most of the contents of their knapsack into their stomachs. And filled with the remains of the previous night's meal, and a helping of porridge as well, they slept in the sand beside the rocking ocean.

Thor and Loki, Thialfi and Roskva did not have to walk far along the strand next morning before they found an old boat, beached and disused. They took it over and hauled it down to the water. Every time Thor pulled the oars the boat reared and kicked forward and by midday they reached the shore of Utgard, a broad strip of land that lay between the water and the mountains.

The four travellers beached their boat and, as there was no sign of life along the coast, they headed inland. After a while they came to a forest that stretched so far in both directions that there seemed to be no way round it. So they made their way into it and began to pick their way through it. All afternoon they walked through the shadows, light-headed with hunger and the sweet-smelling pine; the ground was springy underfoot.

By the time the light began to fade, late in the evening, they had still seen no sign of life and knew that they would have to go without much food that day, for their own stocks were running low.

'We must find somewhere to stay for the night,' said Loki. 'I wouldn't care to end up as carrion.'

'Is Fenrir's father so afraid of wolves?' said Thor, and smiled to himself.

Restless and fleet of foot, Thialfi ran ahead again and again, scouting out the forest. Now he came back with the news that he had found a glade not far ahead, with a curious kind of hall standing in the middle of it. When they reached the glade, Thor and Loki walked round the hall. It puzzled them too. Although there seemed to be no door, the whole of one end of the hall was open; the opening was as high as the hall was high and as wide as it was wide. And the hall itself was enormous; any of the halls in Asgard, even Valhalla, could have fitted inside it.

'This place will keep the rain off our backs,' said Loki. 'And here at least the damp will not seep into our bones.'

The gods and Thialfi and Roskva were so worn with travelling all day that, hungry though they were, they very quickly settled and fell asleep.

At midnight, however, all four of them were shocked out of their sleep. They heard a terrible growling. The noise grew louder, it grew so loud that the hall began to rock and sway. They started to their feet and the ground shuddered under them.

'An earthquake,' shouted Thor.

Thialfi and Roskva stood wide-eyed; then they hugged one another. 'Let's get out,' said Loki. 'I don't want to be flattened and stiff as a plank.'

At this moment, however, the ground stopped shaking. The earth-thunder ceased as abruptly as it had begun, and the night was as silent as it had been before.

'Outside is no safer than inside,' said Thor.

'There must be somewhere better than this,' replied Loki.

'Let us get the hang of the place,' Thor said. 'Known is always better than unknown.'

So the four of them groped their way towards the far end of the hall. But the darkness seemed to grow thicker and more stifling with every step they took. They did, however, make one find: a smaller side-room led off to the right, about half-way down the vast main hall.

'This is better,' said Thor. 'At least we can make a fight of it here if a man or monster shows its face. Earthquakes, however, are something else.'

So Loki and Thialfi and his sister Roskva felt their way into the pitch dark recess of the side-room, and Thor sat down in the doorway. He gripped the handle of his hammer and vowed to guard them against all-comers. Even now, the travellers did not enjoy unbroken sleep. They were woken several times by a muffled roaring, and lay awake for most of the night in a state of dread.

As soon as it began to get light, Thor cautiously made his way out of the hall. At once he saw a man lying full length in the glade and he was not a dwarf. He was asleep, and in his sleep he suddenly snorted. Then he began to snore, and Thor understood the nature of the noise that he and his companions had heard during the night. He looked at the giant grimly and buckled on the belt given to him by the giantess Grid. He felt his strength grow, and surge like a spring tide within him.

At this moment the giant woke up and, seeing Thor standing almost over him, sprang to his feet. He was as tall as the pine trees around them, and Thor was so taken aback at his height that he did not hurl Mjollnir at him but asked, astonished, 'Who on earth are you?'

'Skrymir,' boomed the giant. 'Big Bloke.'

'No one is going to quarrel with that,' muttered Thor.

'I don't have to ask who you are,' said Skrymir, eyeing Loki, Thialfi and Roskva who had now crept out of their sleeping quarters. 'I know you're Thor. Have you moved my glove?'

Skrymir bent down and picked it up – the glove that Thor and the others had taken for a vast hall. Thor now saw that what they had believed to be the main hall was the cavity for Skrymir's hand and four fingers, and that the side-room was the opening for his thumb.

'What would you say to my company today?' said Skrymir.

'We'd welcome it,' Thor said. 'We're on our way to Utgard.'

'Eat and drink with me first,' said Skrymir.

Thor and his companions were far from unhappy about that, for their own knapsack was almost empty. When they had eaten as much as they wanted, Skrymir said, 'Let's pool our provisions.'

'Very well,' said Thor.

So Skrymir simply dropped their knapsack into his own larger bag, tied it up and slung it over his back. Then he set off through the forest, taking huge strides, so that Thor, Loki and Roskva were soon left behind. Even Thialfi, as fleet of foot as any man in Midgard, was hard put to keep up with him. The travellers, however, could always tell which way to go by stopping to listen to the sound of Skrymir crashing through the forest ahead of them. In the evening, they caught up with the giant at the very edge of the forest. He was sitting under a large oak.

'There are no buildings here,' he said, 'but these oaks will give us shelter for the night. I'm tired after such a trek, and all I want to do is sleep.'

Thor looked pained and Loki ravenous; Thialfi and Roskva thought of their father's farm and their mother's cauldron. 'A lack of meat seems little hardship now,' said Roskva forlornly.

'But you can take my bag,' said Skrymir. 'Prepare yourselves some supper.' Then he lay down and rolled over and, within a minute, he was asleep. The oak tree shook at his snoring, and the birds perched in its branches took themselves off for a better place. Thor grasped the bag of provisions. 'You can make the fire,' he told the others, 'and I'll undo it.'

But that is just what he could not do. The straps keeping the travellers from their supper were as adamant as the rope Laeding that was wound round the wolf Fenrir, and Thor was unable to work a single one loose. His companions each took a turn and the prospect of having any supper that evening slowly receded.

Thor grew more and more frustrated. His beard bristled at the thought that Skrymir had not meant them to be able to open the bag. Then he lost his patience altogether. He gripped Mjollnir with both hands and took a couple of steps forward so that he stood right over Skrymir. Then he brought the hammer down on the giant's forehead.

Skrymir sat up. 'What was that?' he said. 'Did a leaf fall on my head?' He looked around him. 'And you, have you had your supper and are you ready to sleep?'

'As a matter of fact,' said Thor hurriedly, 'we were just about to turn in.' The travellers slowly made their way to the shelter of a second massive oak tree standing near by. They lay down there but, now that Thor's hammer had failed him for the first time since it was forged by Brokk and Eitri, they were all too anxious as well as too hungry to be able to sleep.

At midnight Skrymir was snoring again. The trees near by shuddered, and the ground shook under their bodies. Thor decided he had heard enough. Without a word he got up and quietly made his way over to Skrymir. Then he raised Mjollnir quickly and fiercely, and slammed it down on the middle of the giant's crown. He could feel that the head of the hammer had sunk well into Skrymir's brains.

Skrymir sat up. 'Now what was that?' he said. 'Did an acorn fall on my head?' He looked around him. 'And you, Thor, what are you doing over here?'

'Like you,' Thor said hastily, 'I've just woken up. But it's the middle of the night, and we should both go back to sleep.' As he spoke, Thor backed away and lay down again beside his companions under the second oak. His brows beetled and he vowed to himself that when he got the chance to hit Skrymir again, the giant would see stars and plunge to the depth of Neflheim. He lay very still, waiting for Skrymir to go back to sleep.

Shortly before daybreak, Thor was sure his victim was fast asleep. His ears could scarcely withstand the racket of his snoring. Once more he got up, and quietly made his way over to Skrymir. He raised Mjollnir and, with all his immense might, crashed it into the giant's upturned temple. He buried the whole hammer head in Skrymir's brains; it sank in up to the handle.

Skrymir sat up and rubbed his cheek. 'Are there any birds up there in that tree?' he said. 'Just as I was waking, I thought some droppings fell on to me.' He looked around him. 'And you, Thor, are you well and truly awake?'

Thor was dumbstruck.

'It's time your companions stirred themselves. Tell them to get up and dress. It's not far from here to the stronghold of Utgard.' Skrymir narrowed his eyes. 'I've heard you whispering to each other that I'm no dwarf, but wait until you get to Utgard. You'll see men there much bigger than I am.'

Thor slowly shook his head, and his three companions stirred under their oak, and listened to the giant.

'And let me give you a bit of advice,' said Skrymir. 'Keep your pride for your own kind; keep your mouths shut. Utgard-Loki's men won't stand for bragging from small fry like you.'

Thor seethed at such an insult, but there was nothing whatsoever he could do about it. He stood and listened.

'Your other course of action,' said Skrymir, 'would be to head straight home and, in my view, that would be the right one. But if you insist on going on, walk east from here.' Skrymir pointed out the way. 'As for me, I have to head north for those distant mountains.'

Then Skrymir picked up his bag of provisions, threw it over his back and, without a friendly word, without even a nod, he stumped away along the hem of the wood. Thor and his companions watched him go. 'I don't imagine we'll miss him much,' said Loki. 'We won't long to see him again.'

The four travellers left the forest behind. All morning they walked until it was no more than a blur on the horizon. They pressed on over rising ground and, when the sun stood almost directly overhead, crossed a saddle-back indented with three strange square-shaped valleys. Then they climbed down to a plain where stood a massive fortress with soaring walls – the stronghold of Utgard.

Thor and his companions were happy to be near their journey's end. They hurried along a well-worn track that led up to the great gates fashioned from wrought iron. But they were locked and no one attended them. They peered through the bars and marvelled at the size of the halls inside the stronghold.

'The bigger they are, the heavier they fall,' said Thor, fingering Mjollnir. But then he remembered Skrymir again and felt uneasy. He rattled the gates but he was unable either to prise them open or to make himself heard.

'Whenever was brawn as good as brain?' said Loki. 'I said you would need sharp wits.' Then he slipped between the bars and stood, grinning, inside Utgard. Slender Roskva and long-limbed Thialfi followed him at once, but Thor had a less easy time of it. In the end, however, he worked his way through: two of the iron bars made way for him.

The travellers made for the huge hall before them. The door was open, and so they walked in. A large number of giants, male and female, old and young, most of them as vast as Skrymir had described, were lounging on the benches lodged against the walls. They stared at Thor and Loki and Thialfi and began to sneer; they ogled Roskva and began to leer. One giant sat alone in a chair at the end of the hall and judging him to be Utgard-Loki himself, Thor and his companions made their way up to him and courteously greeted him.

The giant king took not the least notice. That is to say, he did not look at them but through them. He made no move and he said nothing. Thor frowned and turned to Loki.

Loki yawned.

'Greetings!' repeated Thor much more forcefully, even though the king of the giants was not deaf. 'We have . . .'

'News,' boomed Utgard-Loki, rudely interrupting Thor, 'travels slowly from other worlds. An event, or visit, overtakes word of it.' He smiled a knowing smile. 'Or am I mistaken in taking this whippersnapper to be Thor the Charioteer?'

Thor bridled but, surrounded by giants, he was unable to call the tune.

For the first time Utgard-Loki looked directly at Thor. 'Well, maybe you're stronger than you look,' he said. 'At what skill would you say you excel? And what can your companions do? We never allow anyone to stay with us unless he is master of some craft or pastime.'

Loki was standing a couple of steps behind the others. Seeing that Thor had no answer on the tip of his tongue, he took up the challenge. 'I've a certain gift,' he called out, 'and I'm ready to prove it. There's no one in this hall who can eat faster than I.'

The giant king considered Loki. 'If you're right that will certainly be an accomplishment,' he said. 'We'll put it to the test.' Utgard-Loki looked along the benches and pointed at a giant sitting at the far end of the hall. 'Logi,' he shouted. 'Come up here and pit yourself against Loki.'

Then the giant king's servants carried a trencher into the hall and set it down before the throne. They heaped it with hunks of chopped meat, and it reminded Thor that rather too long had elapsed since they had last eaten. A chair was provided for Loki at one end of the trencher, and for Logi at the other, and at the word from the giant king, they both began to eat.

They gobbled and consumed and devoured. Each of them ate as fast as he could, edging his chair forward as he ate, and they met in the middle of the trencher. Loki had eaten every scrap of meat and left nothing but the bones. But Logi had not only eaten the meat; he had eaten the bones and the trencher as well.

'I would say,' proclaimed the giant king, 'that Loki is the loser.'

An unpleasant shout from his followers indicated that this was what they thought too.

Loki narrowed his eyes and viewed Utgard-Loki with deep mistrust.

'So what can this young lad do?' asked the giant king.

'I'll run a race against anyone you care to name,' said Thialfi.

'That's a singular skill,' said Utgard-Loki, 'and you must be a fine athlete if you think you can outstrip anyone here. We must put it to the test at once.'

Then the giant king and his followers and the four travellers made their way out of the hall to an open place where there was a level of grass that made a good running track.

'Hugi!' called the giant king.

One of the younger giants ambled up to Utgard-Loki.

'You're just the one to run against Thialfi. Go to your marks for the first race.'

Then, on a sign from the giant king, Thialfi and Hugi sprinted over the grass as fast as their legs could carry them. They scarcely seemed to touch the ground. And Hugi reached the end of the track so far ahead of Thialfi that he was able to turn round and welcome him.

'Well, Thialfi,' said the giant king, 'if you mean to win this contest you'll need to exert yourself. I must say, however, that I've never seen a man from Midgard with such a turn of speed.'

Then Thialfi and Hugi made their way back to the start again and, on a sign from the giant king, they sprinted over the grass as fast as their legs could carry them. They scarcely seemed to touch the ground. And by the time Hugi reached the end of the track, Thialfi was tailing him by the distance of a well-drawn crossbow shot.

'Thialfi is certainly fast on his feet,' said the giant king. 'But I think that victory has slipped from his grasp now. The third race will settle things.'

Thialfi and Hugi made their way back to the start once more and, on a sign from the giant king, they sprinted over the grass as fast as their legs could carry them. They scarcely seemed to touch the ground. And this time Hugi ran twice as fast as Thialfi. By the time he got to the end of the track, Thialfi had still not reached the half-way mark.

After this there was no argument. It was agreed that enough ground had been covered to settle the matter.

'Now, Thor,' said the giant king, 'you're well known for your boasting. I've heard that you brag endlessly about this and that and the other. Which of all your skills will you deign to show us?'

'I'll drink,' said Thor. 'And I very much doubt whether anyone here can sink as much as I can.'

'Very well,' said the giant king.

Then the four travellers and all the giants made their way back into the cavernous hall, and Utgard-Loki asked his cup-bearer to fetch the sconce-horn used by all his followers. The cup-bearer put the brimming horn into Thor's hands.

'We think a man who can drain this in one draught is a good drinker.' said the giant king. 'Some men take two draughts to empty it, but no one here is so feeble that he cannot finish it off in three.'

Thor had a look at the horn. He thought he had seen larger, although it seemed a bit on the long side. He was, moreover, very thirsty, for the giant king had not offered him or his companions so much as a drop since they first reached the hall. He raised the horn to his mouth, closed his eyes, and began to swill the liquid down in enormous gulps; and, as he drank, he felt sure that he would drain the whole horn in one draught. But Thor ran out of breath before the horn ran out of liquid. He raised his head, looked into the horn, and was startled to see that the level of the drink was little lower than before.

'You drank plenty,' boomed Utgard-Loki, 'but nothing like enough.'

The Thunder God scowled at the sconce-horn.

'If I'd been told that Thor could only drink that much, I'd never have believed it,' said the giant king. 'Still, I know you'll empty it with your second draught.'

Thor said nothing. He simply raised the horn to his mouth again, and opened his throat and poured a tide of drink down it until he was gasping for breath. But he was still unable to tilt the horn back and drain it. Thor raised his head and peered into the horn. There was now some space between the rim and the drink and it was possible to carry the horn without spilling liquid, but he thought he had made rather less headway with his second draught than with his first.

Utgard-Loki shook his head and sighed. His breath was like an unsavoury warm wind swirling around Thor and Loki and Thialfi and Roskva. 'What's going on, Thor?' he asked. 'Haven't you left rather too much for comfort? It seems to me that if you're going to empty this horn, your third attempt will have to be your best.'

Thor glared at the sconce-horn and his red beard bristled.

'I know you're much admired in Asgard. But you won't be admired here, you know, not unless you do better in some other contest than you've done in this one.'

Thor was fretful at his own shortcoming and wrathful at the giant king's words. He raised the horn to his mouth, and opened his throat and drank and drank. He drank as much as he could stomach, and still he could not drain it. At last he raised his head and peered into the horn; and he saw that it was at least somewhat lower than before. Then Thor thrust the horn into the cup-bearer's hands, and angrily shook his head at the laughing invitations from all around him to drink more and drink again.

'It's clear enough,' remarked the giant king, 'that your prowess is not all we supposed. Still, do you want to try your hand at some other kind of contest? Your drinking doesn't really do you much justice, does it?'

'I can prove myself in countless ways,' Thor said gruffly. 'But let me say I'd be surprised if anyone in Asgard called such huge draughts trifling.'

Utgard-Loki smiled down at Thor and said nothing.

'So what have you got in store for me now?' said Thor.

The giant king shook his head and sighed. 'Young giants here perform the feat of lifting my cat from the ground. I can't pretend it's very highly rated. Indeed, I'd never have dreamed of suggesting it to mighty Thor unless I'd seen with my own eyes that you're not half as strong as I thought you were.'

As if it had been waiting on its master's words, a grey cat under the giant king's throne uncoiled itself and sprang on to the floor. It was no kitten.

Thor stumped forward, put one massive arm under the cat, and began to lift. As he lifted, the cat simply arched its back. Now Thor used both hands and heaved. But the animal only arched its back still more so that its body formed a steep rainbow over the god's head; its four feet remained on the ground.

All the watching giants laughed at the way in which the cat, with its effortless movement, frustrated Thor's muscular attempts on it. Now Thor stood under the cat, between its legs, and rocked forward on to his toes in an attempt to lift it. And when he stretched his hands and the cat's belly as high above his head as he could, the cat was finally obliged to raise one paw. That was as much as Thor could manage.

'Much as I thought,' said Utgard-Loki. 'It's rather a big cat, and Thor is a midget compared to the mighty men at this court.'

'Call me what you like!' shouted Thor. 'But just let someone come and wrestle with me here. Now I'm really angry.' The Thunder God glared at the giants around him. He was beside himself with his own failures and the giant king's string of taunts and abuses.

Utgard-Loki looked along the benches and rubbed his bush of a beard. 'I can't say I see anyone here to wrestle with you,' he said. 'They'd all feel it was beneath them.'

Now Thor was wondering how he could bring Mjollnir into action. He fingered the hammer and grated his teeth.

'Wait!' said the giant king. 'I've an idea. Go and find Elli, my old foster-mother. Thor can wrestle with her if he wants to.'

The giants chuckled.

'She's thrown men who have struck me as stronger than Thor,' said Utgard-Loki.

After a little while, a horrible old crone hobbled into the hall and made her way towards the throne. The giant king got up to greet his foster-mother and asked her if she would consider coming to grips with Thor.

Elli agreed and threw away her stick. Then Thor fairly hurled himself at the old woman. But the moment he laid hands on her he knew she was far stronger than she seemed. Thor heaved and strained and grunted and the old woman stood firm and unshaken; the greater his pressure, the more easily she withstood it.

Now Elli won the upper hand and tried a hold or two. Suddenly she took Thor by surprise. She caught him in a lock and threw him off balance. Thor bared his teeth and clung to Elli desperately. He tried to take her down with him, but after a struggle, he was forced on to one knee.

'That's enough!' cried Utgard-Loki. 'Quite enough! You've shown us your strength as a wrestler, and there's certainly no need for you to take on any more of my followers.'

After the eating and the running, the drinking and the wrestling, it was late in the evening. Utgard-Loki himself found places for Thor and Loki, Thialfi and Roskva on the crowded benches. And there they were brought as much food and drink as they wished and were made most welcome. Then the floor was padded with bedding and pillows. In that high hall, the four weary travellers and the concourse of giants lay down and fell asleep.

Thor and his companions were the first to wake. They dressed and made ready to leave Utgard. But then the giant king stirred. He picked his way over the trunk-like bodies of his sleeping followers and set up a table beside the travellers. Then he woke his servants and in a little while Thor and Loki and Thialfi and Roskva were regaled once more with food and drink.

Now there was no limit to the giant king's courtesy. He accompanied his guests out of the hall and showed them through the massive gates of Utgard.

For a time they walked across the green plain in the early morning sunlight. The giant king was as genial as can be imagined, but after the previous night's experiences Thor was still chastened and Loki was unusually silent. Thialfi and Roskva, on the other hand, were glad to be away and alive – their spirits rose and they chattered gaily.

'Well,' said Utgard-Loki, 'this is where I must leave you.'

Thor looked up at him.

'How do you feel things have turned out?' asked the giant king. 'Were they as you thought? And tell me, have you ever met anyone more powerful than I?'

Thor shook his head. 'I can't deny,' he said, 'that I've come off second best. You've put me to shame. What's more, I know you'll put it about that I'm nothing to reckon with, and I don't like that.'

'Listen, Thor!' said the giant king. 'I'm going to tell you the truth now that we're outside the walls of Utgard: for as long as I live, and people listen to me, you'll never see the inside of those walls again.'

Thor looked baffled.

'If I'd known how strong you are, you wouldn't have got in at all,' continued Utgard-Loki. 'I can promise you that. Do you know you were very nearly the end of us all?'

Not a word escaped Loki. But he pressed his scarred lips together and began to smile secretly.

'I've used spells to trick you,' said the giant king. 'It was I who met you in the forest. You remember that bag packed with provisions? I fastened it with wires and so it's no wonder you could find no way of undoing it. Then you hit me three times with your hammer. The first blow was the lightest, but if it had touched me, it would have been enough to kill me. That saddle-backed hill not so far from my stronghold, and those three square-shaped valleys, one of them so deep – those were the dents you made with your hammer. I set that saddle-back between you and me, but you never knew it.'

Thor listened to Utgard-Loki's explanation. He listened with mixed feelings: wonder, relief, frustration, and slowly rising anger.

'I used spells, too,' said the giant king, 'when you and your companions competed with my followers. Loki was ravenous and ate very, very fast, but the man called Logi was wildfire itself. He burned up the trencher as well as the meat. And when Thialfi ran against Hugi, he was running against my own thought. He couldn't be expected to keep up with the speed of thought.'

Loki grinned maliciously at Thor. Thor saw nothing to smile about.

'And you,' said the giant king, 'when you drank from that horn you thought you were found wanting. But I tell you, I could scarcely believe my eyes. You didn't realise the other end of the horn was in the sea. When you get back to the ocean, you'll see just how much it has ebbed.' The giant king mused for a while. 'And that cat,' he boomed, 'that was a wonder! Everyone was appalled when you made it lift one paw off the ground. For of course it was not what it seemed to be: it was Jormungand, the Midgard Serpent that encircles the world and bites on its own tail. You reached up so high that it all but grazed its back on the sky.

'And it was a marvel, Thor, that you withstood Elli for so long, and even then only fell on to one knee. Elli is old age. Even if his life is not cut short by the sword or illness or some accident, no one can withstand old age in the end.

'And now,' said the giant king, 'this is where our ways part. It will be better for us both if you do not visit me again. I have used magic, and I'll use it again to protect Utgard so that you'll never be able to harm me in any way.'

Thor was seething. When he heard the giant king's words, he gripped his hammer Mjollnir and raised it over his head. He summoned all his strength.

In vain, all in vain: Utgard-Loki had vanished.

Then Thor swung on his heel with the aim of smashing the walls of Utgard, the halls, the lounging giants. But there was no stronghold there – nothing but a sweeping, shimmering plain. No Utgard; no giant-king; except for the dents in the saddle-backed hill, it was all as if it had never been.

So Thor turned to join his companions. The four of them slowly made their way back to the sea, and crossed it into Midgard. Thor retrieved his chariot and goats from the farmer and his wife. Then, with Loki, Thialfi and Roskva, he returned at last to his hall, galloping over the green and gold fields of Asgard.

THOR GOES FISHING

THE gods had plenty of food but they had run out of mead and ale. They began to feast but the more they ate, the less they felt like eating, with no drink to wash the food down.

They sacrificed a small animal and dipped twigs into its blood. They shook them and the magic signs scored on them began to shine; they shook them again and divined that Aegir, god of the sea, could help them. So a group of gods and goddesses left Asgard and made for the island of Hlesey; and there they found Aegir and his wife Ran in their hall beneath the waves, lit only by gleaming gold.

The sea god was sitting at peace with the world and as blithe as a child. Thor, son of Odin, soon put an end to that. He looked Aegir in the eye and almost blinded him. 'Brew some ale for the gods,' he commanded. 'Brew it at once and brew plenty of it!'

Thor's abrupt tone angered Aegir. He lowered his eyes and considered how to repay him. 'I've no cauldron that would hold enough,' he said. 'Bring me a cauldron, Thor, and I'll brew ale for all the gods.'

The gods and goddesses looked at each other. None of them owned a cauldron that was large enough, nor did they have the least idea where they could get one. Then one-handed Tyr, always truthful, turned to the Thunder God and volunteered, 'My father, the giant Hymir, lives away to the east. I know he has a cauldron – a huge cauldron five miles deep.'

'Do you think we could lay hands on it,' asked Thor, 'this water-whirler?'

'We can,' said Tyr, 'but only if we're cunning. Do not reveal who you are; call yourself Veur.'

So Thor and Tyr set off at high speed and that same day they reached Egil's farm, where Thor once again left his high-horned goats, Tooth-Grinder and Gat-Tooth. Then the gods headed east; they travelled almost to the end of the earth and the sky above, and at last they came to Hymir's hall. It stood on a mountain quite close to the sea.

The first person they came across was Tyr's grandmother for whom Tyr had very little love. She was a monster with nine hundred heads.

Thor shook his head and marvelled greatly.

But then Tyr's mother walked into the hall. She had the most beautiful pale skin and wore a necklace and armbands of gold. She welcomed her son and Thor and brought them goblets of ale. 'Giant blood runs in my veins,' she said. 'I know what's what. Brave as you both may be, I think you'd better hide beneath one of the cauldrons. My husband has rather a brusque way of greeting his guests.'

As might be expected, Thor had little liking for this suggestion, but Tyr sided with his mother and asked Thor what he stood to lose by being a little cautious. And so they waited in safety until ugly Hymir came in late from hunting. As he walked into the hall, the icicles hanging from his frozen beard clinked and chinked.

Hymir's wife got up to meet him. 'Greetings, Hymir! You've got good reason to be happy. Your son is here in the hall – how long we've waited while he journeyed far and wide. And he has brought a companion with him called Veur.' Hymir's gentle wife tried to soften the heart of her husband. 'Look at them sitting at the end of the hall under the gable, hiding behind one of those supports and hoping it will guard them.'

The giant glared balefully at the support and at once the gable's crossbeam cracked. Then eight well tempered cauldrons toppled and fell from the shelf there: they crashed on to the hall floor and smashed into smithereens. Only one did not break, the one under which Thor and Tyr were sheltering.

The two gods crawled out from under the rim and Hymir faced them. The old giant's eyes glittered and he pierced them with his gaze. But when he saw Veur step into the open, he felt uneasy himself and knew no good could come of his visit. All the same, he made due provision for his guests; he gave orders to his servants that no less than three oxen should be slaughtered and flayed and boiled.

At once his servants lopped off the heads of the cattle and carried them to the cauldron hanging over the fire. The meal was prepared. And before he went to sleep that night Thor astonished Hymir by devouring two whole oxen.

Hymir said, 'If the three of us want to eat again together, we'll have to go out hunting.'

'Let us go out rowing, then, and see what we can get,' said Veur
to the savage giant. 'All I need from you is bait.'

'Help yourself from the pasture where my herd is grazing,' said
Hymir. 'I've no doubt, giant killer, that you'll find a turd or two
there easily enough.'

The god at once made his way out of Hymir's hall into the steep
pasture surrounding it. There he found a splendid black ox, Heaven
Bellower. Thor grabbed its high horns and wrenched them apart
until they snapped, and then he broke the beast's neck. 'What you
ate was bad enough,' said Hymir grimly. 'But it seems to me that
you're even more of a nuisance left at large than sitting by my fire.'

Hymir and Thor left the others behind in the hall and went down
to the sea. They launched the giant's boat and, to begin with, Thor
manned the oars. Then Hymir took over. The giant, kinsman of apes,
rowed well out from the land and then shipped his oars so that he
could start to fish.

'Further!' urged Thor. 'Row further!'

'I don't want to row one stroke further,' Hymir replied.

The fierce giant began to prepare his tackle. He fixed hooks to his
line and cast it over the gunwale. Almost at once the line tightened

and Hymir hauled up two whales, hissing and sighing and churning
the water into a maelstrom.

Thor was sitting in the stern, and he prepared his gear with great
care. The slaughterer of monsters and guardian of men baited his
hook with the head of the ox Heaven Bellower. Then he cast his line
into the dark water.

Under the waves the enemy of the gods, the serpent surrounding
Midgard, let go of its own tail and gaped and took the bait.

Thor did not flinch. Fist over fist, he quickly pulled in his line.
Jormungand, the Midgard Serpent, lashed the sea into a frenzy. The
water fizzed and frothed but the Thunder God did not loosen his
grip. He dragged the monster up under the keel and then began to
haul it over the gunwale.

Then Thor raised his hammer and it sang a grisly song on the
hairy head of that terrible serpent, Fenrir's sibling.

The serpent roared and the mountains of Jotunheim heard and
replied. Midgard shuddered. Jormungand tugged at the great barb
piercing the roof of its mouth. It twisted and wrenched and, at last,
with a tearing of flesh, it set itself free; the serpent sank once more
to the bottom of the sea.

Hymir was appalled by what he had seen. He had no heart for
words and made heavy weather of the homeward journey. First he

pulled strongly on one oar, then on the other, in the hope of picking up a following wind to carry them closer to land and into calmer water. When the keel finally scraped the shingle, and the boat lodged, Hymir said, 'There's enough work here for two pairs of hands. Will you drag the boat up beyond the tide mark and secure it? Or would you rather pull the whales back to my hall?'

Without even bothering to reply, Thor stood up and stepped out of the boat. He grabbed the prow with his massive fists and began to raise it – the bilge water slopped and swilled back to the stern. Then the god began to drag the boat with the two whales, the oars and the great bailer still inside it; he hauled it across sand, on through a birch wood, and over a hill until he reached Hymir's hall.

Tyr and his mother welcomed them there, and marvelled at Thor's feat in bringing the boat and the cargo up from the sea.

Even now, stubborn Hymir would not own that he had come off second best, and he resolved on another test of strength. 'You're a fair oarsman, certainly,' he said, 'but so are many others. I'd only call a man strong if he were able to smash this glass goblet.'

Thor took the goblet from Hymir and promptly hurled it against one of the stone pillars supporting the gable. The hall was filled with bits and pieces of flying masonry. Then one of the giant's servants hurried down to the end of the hall and picked up the goblet from a heap of rubble. It was unbroken and he brought it back to Hymir.

Hymir's wife bent her head towards Thor. 'Throw it at his head,' she whispered. 'He eats so much that it's almost solid. However hard that glass is, his head must be harder.'

Then Thor stood up again. He turned to face Hymir and, with all his divine strength, threw the goblet straight at the giant's forehead. Hymir's skull remained intact; but the wine goblet fractured and fell to the floor in two pieces.

Hymir bent down and picked them up and put them on his knees and stared at them. 'With the loss of this goblet,' he said sadly, 'I lose far more than a goblet.' The giant shook his head as if suddenly all his strength had ebbed from him. 'What's mine is yours now. My last cauldron is yours,' he said. 'I can't stop you from taking it. Even so, it will be a mighty task to cart it out of this hall. I'll never be able to say again, "Brew for me cauldron, cauldron, brew me ale!" '

Tyr did not need to be invited twice. He jumped up and took hold of the cauldron and began to pull, but he was unable to move it.

Hymir looked at him and smiled sourly.

Then Tyr tried again. He filled his lungs and pulled, but the cauldron only rocked and settled back into its original position.

Now Thor seized the rim. The cauldron was so massive and Thor exerted so much pressure that his feet splintered the wooden planks and broke right through the hall floor. Then the god hoisted the vast cauldron on to his shoulder and strode out of the hall. Its handles yapped at his ankles.

Thor and Tyr had not gone far before Thor turned round, wanting to have a last look at Hymir's hall. It was just as well that he did. The first thing he saw was Hymir and a whole throng of many-headed giants who had left their lairs in the east and were coming after them. Thor eased the massive cauldron from his shoulder and set it down on the ground. Then his hands were free to take a grip on Mjollnir. He stood his ground and swung his hammer; not a single monster, not one prowler of the wilderness, was able to withstand it.

Now Thor shouldered the cauldron again and the two gods hurried on. It was not long before they reached Egil's farm, where Thor had left his chariot and goats.

Thor returned home while the gods were meeting in solemn assembly at the Well of Urd, under the branches of Yggdrasill. All the gods gazed at the cauldron, amazed; and they acclaimed Thor and his companion Tyr.

So Aegir was outwitted. Thor gave him the cauldron and took away his pride. And that winter and every winter the gods drank tides of warming ale brewed for them in the sea god's gleaming hall.

THOR'S DUEL
WITH HRUNGNIR

ODIN, god of gods, was not content with being able to see everything that happened in the nine worlds. He was not content even with being able to understand all that he saw. His blood raced and he longed to test life's winds and tides for himself.

While Thor was away fighting trolls and troll women and their wolfchildren in Iron Wood, Odin bridled at his own lack of action. He became so restless that he donned his golden helmet and leaped on to Sleipnir, hungry for some happening.

Sleipnir vaulted the torrent beside Valhalla and then the old river that snaked through a canyon; he spring-heeled over the broad gleaming river and the river teeming with spears, and his eight hooves clattered as he galloped over scree. For hour after hour Odin rode towards Jotunheim across utterly dreary country, at first flat and tussocky and pocked with small deserted lakes, then flat and stony — a sea of slabs where nothing lived and nothing grew. At last, where the land began to swell and in some places to smoke, leavened by fires far below the earth crust, Odin came to the hall of Hrungnir, strongest of all the giants.

'Who are you?' demanded Hrungnir.

The One-eyed god pulled his blue cloak close about him, tilted his wide-brimmed hat forward, and said nothing.

'I've been watching. I saw you coming, your golden helmet flashing under the sun. You seemed to be riding as much through the air as on the ground.' Hrungnir rubbed his enormous nose. 'That's an uncommonly fine horse you've got there.'

'Better than any in Jotunheim,' retorted Odin. 'That's for sure.'

'That's what you think,' replied the giant.

'That's what I know,' said Odin.

'What do you know of Jotunheim, little man?' said Hrungnir, his temper rising. 'Don't be so certain.'

'I'm certain enough to wager my head on it.'

'You fool!' bellowed Hrungnir. 'Have you never heard of Gold Mane?'

'Who?' said Odin.

'My horse!' shouted Hrungnir. 'Gold Mane. Fast as your horse may be, Gold Mane will gallop him into the ground.'

'Gab!' spat Odin. 'All gab!'

'Gold Mane!' boomed Hrungnir, and his voice bounced back off the mountain wall.

'My head, Hrungnir,' called Odin, spurring Sleipnir into a gallop. 'Come and collect it!'

By the time Hrungnir had sprung on to Gold Mane, the One-eyed god was already on the other side of the smoking hill. The god and the giant raced across the flatlands and neither gained ground on the other; they raced into the uplands, and Hrungnir had no thought for anything but the chase; they crossed the nineteen rivers and before the thick-headed giant had taken stock of where he was, he found himself inside the walls of Asgard. Then at last he realised who his visitor had been.

Odin was waiting for Hrungnir beside the outer gate of Valhalla. 'That's an uncommonly fine horse you've got there,' he said.

Hrungnir glared at Odin, angry but unable now to do anything about it.

'You must be thirsty after such exertion,' Odin said. 'Let Gold Mane drink from this torrent. And you, Hrungnir, come and drink in Valhalla.'

Odin led the way in under the roof of shields and spears, and his wolves Freki and Geri at once got up and loped towards him. Ranks of warriors filled the benches, feasting and drinking after the day's slaughter, and when they saw the giant, they began to shout. It was an awesome noise, as if the sea itself were caught in the mighty hall and waves were breaking on a strand of stones.

The Father of Battle raised one hand and as the clamour began to die down he called out, 'Hrungnir comes unarmed. He comes in peace. Let him drink and leave in peace.'

'How can I drink,' said Hrungnir, 'without a horn in my hands?'

Then the Valkyries Axe-Time and Raging brought out the two massive horns from which Thor was used to drink. Both were brimming with ale.

'Drink!' said Odin. 'Test your thirst against our finest trenchermen.'

All the company in Valhalla watched as Hrungnir tossed off one horn without taking a breath, and then did the same with the other – such a tide of ale that even Thor might have had trouble with it. It was not long before the giant began to feel the effects. 'I will!' he shouted suddenly.

Odin looked at Hrungnir and his one eye glittered. 'Surely not,' he murmured.

'I will,' the giant shouted again. He waved his arms and, thrusting his head forward, glared at Odin. 'I'll pick up this piffling hall and carry it home to Jotunheim.'

The warriors sitting at the benches roared with laughter. Hrungnir swung round to face them. He meant to take steps towards them, but his balance was wrong and he reeled sideways. 'I'll shink Ashgard in the shea,' he bellowed.

Odin folded his arms. His mask-like face hid his thoughts. After a while he asked rather casually, 'Then what is to become of us?'

'You,' shouted Hrungnir. 'I'm going to kill you, you gods and warriors. Shmash you!' The giant brought his fist down on a trestle table; its end leaped up and the table danced and fell flat on its face.

There was not so much noise in the hall then. Everyone was watching Hrungnir. 'All except you two,' said the giant, pointing at Freyja and Sif, fairest of the goddesses. 'I'll take you back with me. I can find a use for you.'

Odin nodded and Freyja sidled forward. As she moved, all the jewels she was wearing flashed and glimmered, and Hrungnir tried to rub the stars out of his eyes. 'Drink again,' said Freyja. She poured a lot more ale into one of the horns.

'Is jat all the ale in thish hall?' demanded the giant. 'I'll drink every drop of ale in Ashgard.'

But although the giant drank more and more, he did not fall into a stupor as Freyja had planned; he simply assaulted the company with a stream of boasts. The gods and warriors soon became tired of them and Odin sent a messenger to find Thor in Iron Wood and ask him to return to Asgard at once.

* * *

It was not at all long before Thor burst into the hall, swinging his hammer. 'What's this?' he shouted. 'What's next?' No one had seen him more angry, even when Loki had cut off Sif's hair. 'What's next when sly devils of giants can hope to drink in Valhalla?'

Hrungnir looked at Thor blearily, and hiccupped.

'Who says you can drink here?' demanded Thor. 'And why is Freyja waiting on you? Is this a feast in honour of giants?'

The giant waved an arm in the direction of Odin. 'His shafe con-juct,' he burbled. 'Ojin, he invited me in.'

'Less easy to get out again,' said Thor, tightening his hold on his hammer.

'If you kill me unarmed,' said the giant, 'it won't add much to your fame – except for foul play.' Drunk as he was, he well under-stood he still had to escape from Valhalla unscathed and he knew, too, what would touch Thor most closely. 'It would be a better tesht,' he began, 'a much better tesht of your bravery.'

'What?' said Thor.

'If you dared to fight me.'

'Dared,' repeated Thor between his teeth.

'I challenge you to meet me,' said Hrungnir. 'On the borders of Jotunheim and Ashgard. We'll fight at the Stone Fence House.'

Thor looked at the giant and saw that he was in earnest.

'What a great fool I am to have left my hone and shield at home,' said Hrungnir. 'If I had my weapons, we could shettle the matter here and now. But if you mean to kill me unarmed, you're a coward.'

No one had dared challenge Thor to a duel before and the Thunder God was eager to accept. 'You can count on it,' he told the giant. 'I do not break faith. Do not break faith with me.'

Then Hrungnir barged out of Valhalla without a backward look. He heaved himself on to Gold Mane's back and galloped away to Jotunheim as fast as he could.

When the giants heard about Hrungnir's journey to Valhalla and his forthcoming duel with Thor, they thought he had won great honour. 'And,' they said, 'you have won the first part of a famous victory.' But for all that the giants were uneasy and anxious. They knew that if Hrungnir lost the duel, and was killed, it would be a bad hour for Jotunheim. 'If you do not win,' they said, 'what hope is there for us? You're the strongest of us all.'

*   *   *

At the Stone Fence House there was a river with a bed of clay.

'Let us dredge it,' said the giants. 'Let us mould a man so vast that Thor will shake at the sight of him.'

Then the giants worked night and day and piled up the clay and made a mountain of a man: he was nine leagues high, and measured three leagues across the chest from armpit to armpit.

'He may be so tall that the clouds gather round his head,' said the giants, 'but he is nothing but clay. What are we going to do about his heart?'

The giants were quite unable to find a heart anything like large enough. In the end they killed a mare and put her heart into his body. Its pump was enough to give the clay life, but rather too unsteady to inspire much confidence. They called this clay giant Mist Calf, and told him to wait by the river.

On the appointed day Hrungnir headed for the Stone Fence House. And unlike Mist Calf, his heart gave others heart. It was made of unyielding stone, sharp-edged and three-cornered. Hrungnir's head was made of stone, too, and so was the great shield he held in front of him as he waited for Thor. With his other hand, he grasped a huge hone; he shouldered it and was ready to hurl it. Hrungnir looked very nasty and very dangerous.

Then Thor, the Thunder God, angrily sprang into his chariot and Thialfi leaped in beside him. It rocked beneath them. The Charioteer bawled and at once his two goats strained at their harnesses; the chariot rattled out of Asgard. The moon's path quivered and echoed. Lightning flared and flashed and men on middle earth thought the world itself was about to catch fire. Then hail lashed the ground; it smashed frail stooks and flattened fields of grass and men quailed within their walls. Headlands were shaken by such storms that gullies and rifts and gashes and chasms opened underfoot, and rocks and boulders cascaded into the curdling sea.

The god and his servant rolled into Jotunheim towards the Stone Fence House. Then Thialfi jumped out of the chariot and ran ahead of it until he could see Hrungnir and Mist Calf. They stood side by side, and Mist Calf's heart thumped inside him.

'Thor can see you,' shouted Thialfi. 'Can you hear me? Thor can see you with your shield raised before you.' Thialfi cupped his hands to his mouth. 'Can you hear me, Hrungnir? Put it on the ground. Stand by your shield. Thor will come at you from below.'

Then Hrungnir laid his stone shield on the ground and stood on it; he grasped his hone with both hands.

The moment he saw Hrungnir standing at the Stone Fence House, Thor brandished his hammer and hurled it at him. The giant was assaulted by blinding forked flashes and claps of thunder.

Hrungnir saw the hammer flying towards him. He drew back his hone and aimed it straight at Mjollnir. The hammer and the hone met in mid-air with a dazzling flash, followed by a crack that was heard through the nine worlds. The hone was smashed into hundreds of fragments.

The shrapnel flew in every direction. One piece flew to Midgard and splintered again as it crashed into the ground – and every bit is a whetstone quarry. Another piece whistled through the air and lodged in Thor's head. The strongest of all the gods was badly wounded. He fell out of his chariot, and his blood streamed over the earth. But Thor's hammer found its target. Despite the hone, Mjollnir still struck Hrungnir on his forehead and crushed his skull. The giant tottered and fell. One of his massive legs pinned Thor down by the neck.

When Mist Calf saw Thor, he was terrified; he sprang a leak and peed uncontrollably. Then Thialfi swung his axe and attacked Mist Calf, the giant with feet of clay. Thialfi hacked at his legs and Mist Calf did not have enough strength in his body to fight back. He lurched and toppled backwards, and his fall shook Jotunheim. Every giant heard him fall; they knew what had happened at the Stone Fence House.

'My head!' growled Thor.

Thialfi inspected the piece of whetstone stuck in Thor's head.

'It's in better shape than Hrungnir's head,' said Thialfi. He seized the giant's leg and tried to lift it and release Thor. But for Thialfi it was like trying to lift the trunk of a tree; he was unable to move it an inch.

'Get help,' said Thor.

Thialfi put his fleetness of foot to good use. It was not at all long before many of the gods hurried out of Asgard and came to the Stone Fence House, rejoicing at Thor's great victory and anxious to release him. One by one the strongest of the gods tried to lift the giant's leg but none of them – not even Odin himself – was able to do anything about it.

The last to reach Stone Fence House was Magni, the son of Thor and a giantess. He was three years old. When he saw how the gods were unable to release his father, he said, 'Now let me try!' Magni stooped, grasped Hrungnir by the heel, and swung the giant's foot away from his father's neck.

All the gods cried out in wonder and Thor quickly got to his feet.

'It's a pity I didn't come sooner,' said Magni. 'If I had met this giant, I'd have struck him dead with my bare fist.'

'If you go on as you've begun,' said Thor warmly, clamping an iron-gloved hand on to his son's shoulder, 'you'll become quite strong.'

'My mother is Iron Cutlass,' Magni said. 'And I am the son of Thunder.'

'What's more,' said Thor, 'I'm going to give you Gold Mane. Take Hrungnir's horse as a reward.'

'No,' said Odin sharply. 'You shouldn't give such an uncommonly fine horse to this son of a giantess; give it to your own father.'

Thor took no notice. He clapped his hands to his banging head and rode back to Asgard, followed by the Aesir. Only Odin complained; the other gods gave thanks that good had prevailed over evil and that they seemed quite safe again, as safe as they had ever been.

When Thor reached his own hall, the whetstone was still stuck in his head. So he sent to Midgard for the wise woman Groa, the wife of Aurvandil the Brave. Groa hurried up over Bifrost and all night she chanted magic words over Thor – charms and spells known only to her. As she sang, the hone began to work loose, and the hammering in Thor's head began to fade. It seemed less like pain than the memory of pain.

Thor was so thankful that he wanted to make Groa happy. 'I have a surprise for you,' he said.

'Nothing could surprise me,' said Groa.

'This will,' said Thor. 'Not long ago I was in the north and I met your husband, Aurvandil the Brave.'

Groa stiffened. Then she began to shake her head sadly.

'You may think he's dead,' said Thor, 'but I brought him out of Jotunheim. I waded across the streams of venom carrying him in a basket strapped on to my back.'

'Stuff!' said Groa gruffly, not because she wanted to disbelieve Thor but because she did not dare to believe him.

'Do you need proof?' asked Thor.

'Yes,' said Groa.

'All night you've sung charms over my head,' said Thor, 'and it is almost morning. Come with me.' The Thunder God led the way out of his hall into the silent courtyard. 'Look!' said Thor, pointing into the sky. 'Have you ever seen that star?'

Groa frowned and shook her head.

Thor smiled faintly. 'One of Aurvandil's toes stuck out of the basket, and froze. So I broke it off and hurled it into heaven. Now and always that star will be known as Aurvandil's Toe.'

Groa's heart was pounding; her eyes shone with tears of joy.

'Now are you satisfied?' said Thor. 'And I'll tell you one thing more. It won't be long at all now before your husband gets home.'

Groa felt as if nothing else in the world had ever mattered; and she felt as if there were no way in which she could properly thank Thor.

'Only finish your charms and spells,' said Thor. 'Then I too will be happy.'

Groa looked at Thor and gaped.

'The charms,' said Thor.

The wise woman's head whirled and her blood raced round her body. She was so excited that she could not recall a single charm.

'Think, woman!' said Thor fretfully.

Groa buried her face in her hands but it was no good.

'Think, woman, think!' roared Thor. His eyes blazed and his red beard bristled.

But Groa was able to think only of her husband Aurvandil's homecoming, and of a shining star. Thor sent her packing with a bellow of fury. And that is why the whetstone remained in Thor's head.

GYLFI AND GEFION

'YOU have treated me like a king,' said Gylfi.
The wizened beggar-woman sat in her cocoon of filthy, reeking rags and listened.

'Our bed was only this bare ground,' said Gylfi, 'and our roof was only this whispering tree and the litter of stars beyond. But all that you had to share – your scraps of food, your store of understanding – you willingly offered.'

The beggar-woman's eyes were deep wells, unfathomable and strangely gleaming.

'You have treated me like a king,' Gylfi said, 'and now I want to tell you that I am the king.'

The beggar-women looked at Gylfi without changing her expression. She sniffed.

'As you shared with me, I will share with you,' said Gylfi. 'You're welcome to as much of Sweden as you can plough with four oxen in one day and one night.'

Then the king and the beggar-woman went their own ways. Gylfi, found and followed a track out of the forest and came back to his court. The beggar-woman, none other than the goddess Gefion, left Midgard and journeyed into Jotunheim.

Gefion walked past cauldrons of mud and boiling springs, she worked her way round the base of a mountain and reached a secluded fertile valley. No man lived there, but four huge oxen were grazing under the hot sun – the four sons of the goddess and a giant.

Gefion took her sons with her back to Midgard and into the country of Sweden. She chose a piece of land, very fine to look at and even better for farming, and yoked the four oxen to a massive plough. The coulter bit so deep that it began to loosen the crust of the earth. Now the oxen strained with every sinew and muscle and wrenched the mould away from the molten rock beneath.

Gefion laughed as her four sons dragged off a great piece of land. The oxen slowly made their way westward. They reeked with sweat. The goddess urged them on and they waded into the sea, still hauling the land behind them, until at last they stopped in the middle of a sound.

'Leave the land here,' Gefion said. 'Let it lie here until the end of the world!' She unyoked the oxen from the plough, oxen with eyes like moons not unlike their mother. 'And let this fertile island be known as Zealand,' said the goddess.

So Gefion repaid Gylfi's generosity by looting his land. That which made Denmark larger made Sweden smaller. Water oozed from the earth and fell from the sky into the gaping wound where the land had been ripped up, and it became a lake. Men called it Mälar.

And that is why the headlands of Zealand fit the inlets and the bays and the bights of Lake Mälar.

THOR AND THE FERRYMAN

A RANK of mountains stood behind Thor. Some were like upturned ships, some like unfinished pyramids and monstrous cones with their tops sawn off, and none of them were smiling.

Thor strode west over the tundra, and the sun kept pace with him. Then late in the morning he left the wilderness behind him and hurried across scrub and undulating land.

So he came to a sound, a swift deep channel. The air was utterly still there. The sun placed a dazzling hand on the water, and the water seemed barely to move as it moved.

On the far bank a figure sprawled on his fine cloak in the midday sun, and his flat-bottomed boat lounged beside him.

'Hey!' bawled Thor, and the water quivered. 'You over there. Are you the ferryman?'

The figure stirred and sat up. He cupped his hands. 'Who is that oaf yelling over the water?'

'Ferry me across,' called Thor. 'I'll pay you well from this panier.' Thor eased his thumbs under the shoulder straps. 'It's packed out with fine fare, and I've eaten as much as I can already. I had a glut of herrings and a pool of porridge before I set out.'

The ferryman slowly got to his feet and pulled his wide-brimmed hat well down over his one eye. 'You're pleased with yourself, aren't you? Ah! If only you knew what lies in store for you. When you near home, you'll hear nothing but moans. Your mother is dead.'

'My mother dead!' cried Thor. He screwed up his eyes; he screwed up his whole face. 'What grief could be greater?'

Having alarmed and upset the credulous Thor, the ferryman began to insult him. 'Barefoot,' he called scathingly. 'Beggar's clothes. Not even breeches. I doubt if you even have a place you can call your own.'

'Bring over your boat,' roared Thor. 'No need to be afraid: I'll guide you in. Anyhow whose ferry is that?'

Now the ferryman took his time; he turned his back on Thor to taunt him, and smiled grimly.

'Whose ferry is that?' repeated Thor.

'Hildolf, the slaughtering wolf, entrusts it to me. He's a wise man. And he has given me my orders: no pilferers, no horse thieves; only worthy men and well known faces. So,' said the ferryman, 'if you want to cross here, tell me your name.'

'I'll tell you,' shouted Thor, 'though I stand alone. I am Odin's son, strongest of the gods. You, ferryman, you're talking to Thor.' The god's words made waves on the sound; they ran straight across the channel and broke at the ferryman's feet. 'And who are you, I'd like to know?' shouted Thor. 'Tell me your name, ferryman.'

'My name is Harbard; I seldom hide it.'

'Why should you hide it? Or am I talking to an outlaw caught up in some feud?'

'What if you are?' retorted the ferryman. 'Unless I'm fated, I can look after myself against the likes of you.'

Thor clenched his right fist, rubbed it against his beard and stared at the cold water. 'You're not worth the trouble of wading across this channel and getting soaked up to the waist. But I'll repay you, you knock-kneed ferryman, when I get across this sound!'

Harbard put his hands on his hips. 'Here I stand and here I'll wait. You've not met my equal since you fought Hrungnir.'

'You want to talk about Hrungnir, do you? That lolloping giant! His head was made of stone and yet I killed him, I laid him out lifeless. And you, Harbard, what were you doing meanwhile?'

'I spent five winters on the island of Algron. There was plenty to do. There I fought. There I made love.'

Thor rubbed his beard again. 'How did you win them, your women?'

'They welcomed me with good grace; yes, with high spirits. And they were well advised to do so, for they could no more have escaped me than make ropes of sand or dig the bottoms out of valleys.' Harbard opened his arms. 'I was the one they turned to first. I slept with seven sisters, and each one gave me ecstasy. And you, Thor, what were you doing meanwhile?'

'I killed the fierce giant Thiazi and hurled his eyes into scalding heaven. They bear witness to my feats; everyone can see them. And you, Harbard, what were you doing meanwhile?'

'I enticed night riders from their husbands, I wrought love craft with those witches. And that giant Hlebard, he was not made of straw; he gave me a magic branch, and I whipped his wits off him.'

'So,' called Thor, 'that's how you repay a generous gift.'

The grey-bearded ferryman shrugged. 'The oak,' he shouted across the shining water, 'grows strong on shavings from all sides. Each man for himself. And you, Thor, what were you doing meanwhile?'

'I journeyed east to Jotunheim. I slaughtered slovenly giant women as they shambled over the fells. If they were still alive, there would be a terrible throng of giants and no men in Midgard. And you, Harbard, what were you doing meanwhile?'

'I was the cause of war in Valland, the land of slaughter. I set princes at each other's throats. I thwarted peace.'

Thor looked at the ferryman. He listened; his brow was creased in thought.

'After they've fallen in the fight,' shouted Harbard, 'the nobly born journey to Odin. But Thor, he caters for a great gang of thralls.'

'I see how even-handed you'd be in your gifts of men to the gods,' retorted Thor. 'Not that you've any say in the matter.'

'Your limbs are strong but your heart is faint,' jeered the ferryman. 'Such was your fear, you were glad enough once to crawl into a glove, and there you forgot your name. Thunderer? You were so scared Skrymir might hear you that you didn't dare fart or sneeze.'

'You womanish ferryman! I'd swipe you straight down to Hel if I could reach over this sound.'

'Why bother?' said Harbard, with a voice like oil. 'We have no quarrel. And you, Thor, what did you do next?'

'Away in the east, I patrolled the bank of the river Iving. The giant Svarang's sons tried their luck there.' Thor suddenly stopped, and in one movement picked up a block of stone and hurled it over the sound. It whirred as it flew. Harbard stepped hurriedly out of the way and the boulder buried itself in the bank beside him. 'Like that!' yelled Thor. 'They threw boulders; much good it did them! Then they begged for a truce. And you, Harbard, what were you doing meanwhile?'

'I was in the east, too, and came to a certain understanding. I turned the head of a linen-white maid, and we met in secret. I made love to that lady, wearing gold ornaments.'

'A woman well found,' said Thor. 'I wish I'd been with you.'

'And I'd have trusted you,' said Harbard evenly, 'if you were not known for breaking promises.'

'No!' called Thor. 'That's not true. I'm no heel-biter, like an old leather shoe in spring.'

'And you, Thor, what were you doing meanwhile?'

'I was on Hlesey, the island of the sea god. I slew the brides of the Berserks. They were depraved serpents.'

'Thor, you brought shame on your head,' said Harbard scathingly, 'you ladykiller!'

'They were more like wolves than women,' protested Thor. 'They attacked my well trimmed ship and threatened us with iron clubs; Thialfi ran away. And you, Harbard, what were you doing meanwhile?'

'I was one of the host that came to Asgard's frontiers to raise our banners and redden our spears.'

'Are you telling me that you meant to fight the gods?'

'I'll give you a little finger-ring and then you won't fret,' said the ferryman, mockingly. 'It will be a peace-maker between us.'

Thor was enraged. He kicked at the bank and a hailstorm of grit and pebbles ripped the silken water. He gripped Mjollnir in his huge fist. 'Where did you dredge up such filthy abuse? I've never heard so foul an insult.'

'I learned it from men, age-old men who live in the hills of home.'

Thor shook his head in anger and envy. 'That's a fine name for barrows: hills of home.'

'That's what I call them.'

'And your sharp tongue will be the end of you if I choose to wade across this river,' shouted Thor. 'You'll howl more loudly than a wolf if I hit you with this hammer.'

Harbard replied all the more swiftly. 'Your wife, Sif, she's doing some entertaining. She has a lover. Keep your strength for him; that would be more to the point.'

'You witless fool!' roared Thor. 'Shut your mouth and keep your stabbing tongue inside it. You're a liar!'

The ferryman paused and with his one eye peered into the shining water that stops for no man. 'No,' he called, 'I'm telling the truth. Anyhow, how long you're taking to get home! You'd be well on your way by now if you'd crossed in this boat.'

'You womanish ferryman! You've kept me waiting for much too long.' Thor paced up and down the bank of the sound, now swinging round and changing direction, now glaring across the water, like a caged animal. The ferryman watched him. 'I never thought a mere ferryman could detain the god Thor.'

Thor's eyes were blazing and he gave a great bellow that rang round the sky. 'Here's some advice: row your boat straight over; keep your mouth shut; and set down Thor on the far bank.'

'Go away!' retorted Harbard. 'I'm not rowing you across.'

Thor bent over the swift cold water. He saw himself in it, and saw, too, how the ferryman had toyed with him and how, for once, his strength was no use to him. He lifted his head and thrust out his red beard. 'If you won't ferry me over,' he called, 'at least tell me the way round.'

'Few words but many miles,' replied Harbard. 'Over stock and over stone. Take the track on your left until you come to Midgard; and there you'll find your mother. She'll show you the way to the trembling rainbow that brings men to Asgard.'

'Can I get home today?' asked Thor.

'Walk fast, don't rest, and you might be back before sunrise.'

'We've talked long enough,' said Thor angrily. 'You do nothing but mock me.' He turned, and then looked back over his shoulder. 'If we ever meet, I'll pay you in full for refusing me this ride.'

Thor strode away, furious and scorned. And as he went, the jeering laugh of the ferryman followed him. And then Harbard's words: 'Get lost! Let every evil being have you!'

The god quickened into the vast grey wasteland. There was a sandstorm in the wilderness. The wind unwound it, a long scarf leading into the lee of the indigo mountains.

THOR VISITS GEIRROD

'LEND me your falcon skin,' Loki said.

Frigg smiled and nodded; and her maidservant fetched the feather coat and draped it over Loki's shoulders.

'That's the trouble,' said Loki, leering at Frigg. 'These things so easily won, barely worth winning . . .' With that he tied on the skin, and flew round Frigg's hall and out of the door.

The Sky Traveller was bored with the string of days in Asgard that unwound without a knot or a twist in them. He headed for Jotunheim and came to a circle of green fields that he had never seen before. They were enclosed by a jumble of silver and grey rock that stretched for as far as the eye could see. A hall stood there and Loki swooped and settled on a window ledge.

The Sky Traveller peered in and saw a giant and his two daughters feasting in that hall.

The giant, Geirrod, peered out and saw a handsome hawk sitting on the window ledge. 'Catch that bird,' said the giant. 'Bring it to me.'

Loki's eyes gleamed and when one of Geirrod's servants came out of the hall, he flew up to the eaves just out of his reach.

Geirrod's servant got a foothold on the window ledge and stretched out a hand to snare the hawk. But the Sky Traveller had no intention of allowing himself to be caught. He hopped up by the side of the roof, perched on the top, near the chimney hole, and gave a mocking screech. He saw no point in flying off until he had forced the giant servant to climb on to the steep roof where there were no handholds, and risk his life.

Once again the servant reached out and Loki thought it was time to take to the air. He spread his wings, he stood poised. But then, to his dismay, Loki found he was unable to move; his two feet were fixed to the thatch like branches to the trunk of a tree, and Loki knew what kind of a giant it was that he had to deal with. So the servant grabbed the hawk and brought him in to his master, Geirrod.

'I'll put jesses on him,' Geirrod boomed. 'I'll feed him in his fetters, offer him mere morsels until he's trained to my hand.'

The servant gave the hawk into the giant's cupped hands and Geirrod grasped it and looked at it. Loki's eyes were red and green and subtle.

'This is no hawk,' said Geirrod to his daughters, Gjalp and Greip. 'This is some being in disguise. Look at his eyes.' The giant squeezed the bird in his horny hand. 'Who are you?' he demanded.

Loki said nothing.

Geirrod squeezed again until Loki felt that he had been moulded into one solid mass. He gasped and screeched; but still he said nothing.

'Hunger opens the mouth,' said Geirrod, getting up from his seat and striding across the hall. He unlocked a huge chest, thrust the hawk into it, slammed down the lid and locked it again.

For three months Loki sat in darkness. He had nothing to eat; he fouled his own nest; he breathed stale air; he began to feel extremely sorry for himself. And he became so weak from hunger that he could not call out loudly enough to make himself heard; or else, if they did hear him, Geirrod and his daughters chose to ignore him. At the end of three months Geirrod opened the chest and pulled out the hawk. 'Long enough?' was all he said.

The hawk blinked and looked around.

'Not long enough,' said Geirrod.

'Loki,' said the hawk.

'Ah!' exclaimed Geirrod. He took an even firmer grip on his victim. 'Loki,' he repeated, and smiled.

The Sky Traveller looked longingly towards the hall door. But the giant had much too firm a hold on him for any chance of escape.

'Well, Loki,' said the giant, 'do you want to live any longer?'

Loki listened.

'We can make this bargain,' said Geirrod. 'If you swear on oath that you will bring Thor to this hall without his hammer or his belt of strength, I'll spare your life.'

When Loki said nothing, Geirrod began the terrible squeezing again and it was plain that he did not mean to stop. So Loki saw that he had no choice but to agree. He swore to bring Thor to Geirrod's hall. Then Geirrod let Loki eat as much as he wanted. The Sky Traveller scowled at Geirrod and Gjalp and Greip, spread his wings and flew home to Asgard.

Thor and Loki had a great liking for each other's company, and often travelled together through the nine worlds. Once they were walking through the rocky uplands to the east of Asgard and, trusting as he was, Thor suspected nothing when Loki said they need travel only a little further, across green meadows springy underfoot, to visit the giant Geirrod.

Thor said he had never heard of Geirrod.

'He's rather ugly,' said Loki, 'but he has two attractive daughters. He'd like to meet you and you'd like to meet them.'

Thor puckered his mouth, wishing he had brought his hammer Mjollnir and his girdle of strength in case things did not turn out too well.

'What's more,' said Loki, 'we can stay with Grid tonight – her door is always open.'

Thor liked the sound of that.

Thor kept walking and before nightfall Grid welcomed the two of them into her hall.

Not long after supper Loki spread out some straw and fell asleep. In the flickering firelight his expression seemed to change from moment to moment, light and dark, gay and grim.

'Now that Loki is asleep,' said Grid, 'let me tell you the truth about Geirrod.'

Thor looked at the giantess drunkenly.

'Listen!' said Grid. 'Geirrod has little love for the gods, and even less for the god who killed Hrungnir.'

'But that was me!' exclaimed Thor.

'That's what I am saying,' said Grid sharply. 'Listen! Geirrod is as cunning as a fox; he'll be a worthy enemy, even for you. He will let you walk into his hall but arrange for you to be carried out of it.'

Thor wished the ale mist would clear from his head. He kept screwing up his eyes, then opening them wide and rolling them round and round.

'Go if you must,' said Grid, 'but go well armed. I'll lend you my own weapons.' Then the giantess gave Thor her belt of strength, her iron gloves and unbreakable staff.

Thor thanked her and fell asleep.

The next morning Thor and Loki left Grid's hall and continued their journey. Loki looked at Thor's weapons and wondered what Grid had said to him after he had fallen asleep; Thor looked at Loki and wondered how much he knew about Geirrod.

After a while the two gods came to a torrent, a great surge of water broken by worn rocks and grazed by more rock just under the surface; it frothed and hissed as it hurried downstream.

Thor secured the belt of strength and told Loki to hang on to it. Then he grasped Grid's staff and, putting his weight on it, began to wade across the river. The pebbles were slippery underfoot, dogfish tickled his ankles, and Thor was soon in up to his waist; Loki's head was only just above the surface.

By the time the two gods were midstream, Loki had his arms round Thor's neck. The river was breaking over Thor's shoulders and seemed to be rising all the time. Thor cursed and shouted at the river, 'You cannot stop me on my way to the giants. However high you rise, I'll rise higher. I'll rise as high as heaven!'

At that moment, the power of the torrent was so great that Thor was swept off his feet, with Loki still clinging to his neck. As he was carried downstream he grabbed hold of a rowan tree growing in the river, and it held firm in the river bed. Thor recovered his footing, and from there he was able to make his way into the shallows and so, at last, on to the far bank.

'That rowan tree saved our lives,' said Thor.

After a while the two gods went on their way and, late in the afternoon, they reached Geirrod's hall. Geirrod himself was nowhere about but their arrival was clearly expected for a giant servant welcomed them and offered to show them where they would be sleeping.

Thor and Loki readily accepted. They were tired, and caked with mud after their journey.

Then the servant led the gods through the outhouses to a gloomy, rank goat shed. It was furnished with a heap of rotten straw and a single chair. Thor bristled at such an insult; nevertheless he said nothing. He thought he would bide his time until he came face to face with Geirrod himself.

Loki took himself off to wash in the stream that ran past Geirrod's hall, and Thor sat down in the chair. He clenched his fist round Grid's staff, then he yawned. His fatigue got the better of his anger and he began to drowse.

When Thor closed his eyes, it was not long before he imagined he was crossing the river again – losing his foothold, flailing in the water, floating . . . Thor opened his eyes and at once saw the reason for his dream: he was indeed floating once more. He was rising in his chair towards the rafters of the goat shed, and was close to being driven against them, head first.

Thor gripped Grid's staff with both hands. He raised it and rammed it against the roof beam, and pushed with all his strength. He thrust so hard that whatever was beneath him, hoisting him towards the roof, could not resist him and gave way. Thor fell back to the ground with a great crash and screams shook the shed.

Gjalp and Greip, Geirrod's two daughters, had been hiding under the chair when Thor first sat in it, and tried to crush him to death. But they themselves suffered the fate they had planned for the Thunder God. Thor's massive weight was more than their bone-chambers could withstand. Their rib-cages were smashed, their backs were broken, and they died in agony.

It was not long before Loki returned from the stream and, shortly after, the giant servant stood outside the shed and shouted that Geirrod was waiting for Thor in the hall. 'He has it in mind to challenge you to a game or two,' he said.

Thor needed no further warning. He put on Grid's belt of strength and iron gauntlets and then he and Loki made their way back through the outhouses to Geirrod's hall. Thor was surprised to see that there was a string of huge furnaces right down the length of the hall. The turf walls glowed and, lofty as it was, the room was rather too warm for comfort.

Geirrod was waiting for his guest at the far end of the hall. As soon as one of his servants had closed the door behind the gods, Geirrod stepped forward with his hand outstretched.

This was not to greet Thor; it was to pick up a pair of tongs.

Geirrod gripped a large ball of red-hot iron between the tongs. 'Welcome!' he shouted, and hurled the ball straight at Thor.

Thor saw it coming. He dropped his staff, raised both hands and caught the red-hot ball in his iron gloves. He did not move. His eyes flamed, his red beard bristled. Everyone in the hall scrambled under the tables, and Geirrod himself quickly stepped back behind one of the hall supports – an iron pillar.

Then Thor raised his right hand; the ball had begun to smoke. He took one step forward and put all his strength into hurling it down the hall.

The ball punched a hold through the iron support; then it passed through the giant Geirrod's midriff; it punctured the end wall and lodged in the earth slope outside.

Geirrod fell backwards. He hissed as if all the venom bottled inside him were escaping. Then suddenly he gave a violent jerk, gurgled and was dead.

Thor picked up Grid's staff and began to lay about him. While Loki took the chance of slipping out of the hall unnoticed, the Thunder God smashed the skulls of all the dolts who had waited on Geirrod and his daughters.

That was that. Thor strode out of the silent hall and looked at the jumble of rocks around him. He thought he remembered words about green meadows springy underfoot, and talk of two attractive daughters. Thor shook his head and vowed to settle the score with two-faced Loki.

OTTER'S RANSOM

WINTER had lost its heart. Every day the stallions Arvak and Alsvid rose earlier to haul the Sun's chariot across the sky, and quietly the snow pulled back from the valleys and plains of Midgard. Small choirs of birds sang and Odin, Loki and Honir were eager to continue their exploration of the nine worlds.

Early one morning the three gods crossed the flaming rainbow bridge and, talking and laughing, they spring-heeled into Midgard. Odin and Loki had to stretch their legs to keep up with swift Honir.

Suddenly a late snowstorm assaulted the travellers. They shrugged their way through thick wet flakes that tangled and danced and spun and flew in every direction until that wild onslaught ended as abruptly as it had begun; the sun boomed through layers of shapeless cloud, filling it with fierce yellow light; and then there was only the orb of the sun, the expanding acres of pale blue sky, and the blue and green levels of open Midgard.

The three gods followed the course of a river towards its head. And in the afternoon, they walked up under a waterfall. They strode into the thunder, through the spray-diamonds, and stared into the maelstrom.

Then Odin spotted an otter stretched out on the scraggy bank not fifty paces from them; he pointed it out to Loki and Honir. The otter's eyes were shut. Feeling blessed and rather drowsy in the afternoon sun, it had just begun to eat a salmon it had caught in the waterfall.

Loki pursed his lips. He bent down and picked up a fist-sized stone, took aim, and threw it as hard as he could at the otter. The stone hit the animal on the head and killed it outright.

'Well, then,' shouted Loki, struggling back to Odin and Honir with the salmon under one arm and the limp otter under the other, 'what do you say to that? Two for the price of one?'

The three companions were all equally delighted: Loki at his prowess, and Odin and Honir at the prospect of a good meal that evening.

They climbed up the steep bank beside the waterfall and continued on their way up the narrowing river valley.

The sun had already been drawn out of sight, and it was half-way to dark when the gods saw a farm only a little way ahead of them. Smoke lifted from its chimney. They quickened their step and gave thanks for their good fortune.

'Can you give us lodgings for the night?' Odin asked the farmer Hreidmar. 'We've no wish for a dew-bed.'

'How many are you?' said Hreidmar.

'There are two others outside,' Odin replied. 'And we can pay for our beds with food. We were in luck today and there's enough for everyone.'

'For my sons as well?' said Hreidmar. 'For Fafnir and Regin? And for my daughters?'

'Enough for everyone,' said Odin airily.

Then Hreidmar nodded without much enthusiasm, and Odin went to the door and called to Loki and Honir.

'Here we are,' said Honir.

'And here's our supper,' said Loki cheerfully. 'I bagged them both with one stone.'

When Hreidmar saw the otter draped under his nose, he stiffened. For a moment his eyes glazed; then he turned and walked out of the room.

'What's wrong with him?' said Loki.

Odin shrugged. 'A cool welcome is better than a cold night,' he said.

'I'm not so sure,' said Honir.

'No,' Odin replied. 'You never are!'

Hreidmar walked down the low passage, punching the turf walls, and found Fafnir and Regin. 'What do you think?' he said. 'Your brother Otter is dead.'

'Dead?' exclaimed the brothers, leaping up.

'Dead. And what else do you think? His murderers are our guests for the night.'

Fafnir and Regin were outraged and swore to avenge Otter's death.

'There are three of them and three of us,' said Hreidmar, 'so we'll have to surprise them. Each of us must take one when I give the nod. One has rather a fine spear and might be better off without it; and one has strange shoes and could be better off barefoot; I see nothing harmful about the third. I'll use my magic – I'll chant spells to weaken them. I'll sing a charm to bind them.'

Fafnir and Regin did just as their father said. The three of them leaped on to their visitors, and the farmer-magician Hreidmar weakened their resistance so that Odin lost his spear Gungnir, and Loki was relieved of his sky-shoes. When the three gods lay on the ground, bound hand and foot, Hreidmar shouted, 'My son, you've killed my son. I'll kill you all for vengeance. You've killed my son.'

'What does he mean?' asked Odin.

'Otter was our brother,' Fafnir said.

'The finest of fishermen,' said Regin.

'By day,' Fafnir said, 'he had the likeness of an otter. All day he lived in the river and beside the river.'

'And brought his prey to our father.'

'A supply of fresh fish.'

'Our brother.'

'We didn't know this,' said Odin. 'If we had, Loki would never have killed him.'

'Dead is dead.' said Hreidmar.

'We didn't know this,' Odin said again. 'Do you think we'd have come straight to his father's farm? You must as least give us a chance to pay a ransom before killing us.'

Hreidmar looked down at his three visitors and said nothing.

'I speak for the three of us,' Odin said. 'We'll pay as much as you demand.'

Hreidmar thought for a while. 'That would be fair,' he said, 'if you were to keep to your word. You must swear an oath – and if you break it, you will all pay with your heads.'

Then the three companions swore that they would raise as much ransom as Hreidmar asked.

'All right,' said the magician, turning to Fafnir and Regin. 'Where are my daughters? Have them flay Otter and bring me his skin again.'

Fafnir and Regin obeyed their father, and then Hreidmar laid out Otter's handsome skin beside the fire. 'First you must fill this with red gold,' he told the gods, 'and then you must cover it with red gold into the bargain. It must be wholly covered. That is the ransom for the death of my son.'

'So be it,' said Odin. And he rolled over until he was close enough to Loki to whisper in his ear.

Loki listened carefully and then he said, 'Let me go for the gold. Let me go, and hold the other two as hostages.'

So Hreidmar untied Loki's bonds and, with a snatch of a look and a jeering laugh that left Hreidmar and his sons and even Honir uneasy, Loki threw open the door and ran out into the night.

Loki had left his sky-shoes in the care of the magician and, in any event, he was in no great hurry. He knew Hreidmar had nothing to gain by killing Odin and Honir and everything to win by waiting for his return with the red gold; and he was not especially averse to the thought of mighty Odin and long-legged Honir lying for a while, bound hand and foot. So he dawdled all the way across Midgard to the island of Hlesey.

There, Loki visited Aegir and Ran in their hall on the sea bed. 'The gods are in danger,' he told Ran breathlessly. 'Odin himself lies bound, Odin and Honir, and only your net can save them.'

The wife of the sea god opened her cold pale eyes very wide.

'Lend me your drowning net. I can use it, and not to snare men but to save gods.'

When Loki had talked Ran into parting with her net, he left the hall beneath the waves quickly in case she changed her mind, and headed for the world of the dark elves.

Loki picked his way down a chain of dripping tunnels and through a maze of twilit chambers, until he came to a massive cavern. Its roof was supported by columns of rock thicker than tree trunks, and its corners were still and dark. A little light, however, filtered into the middle of the cavern from a vertical shaft in the roof, and showed Loki what he had come to see: a large silent pool, filled with water that seemed to spring from nowhere and flow nowhere.

Loki spread out Ran's finely meshed net and cast it into the pool. He dragged it and pulled it up and there, furiously lashing and writhing, was a large pike snared in the net.

Avoiding its nasty teeth and the equally nasty look in its yellow eyes, Loki took hold of it. 'First,' he said, as he gave the pike a horrible shaking, 'you'll change shape.'

'Change shape,' echoed the cavern.

Then there was no pike but the dwarf Andvari in Ran's dripping net. Loki disentangled him, keeping a firm hold all the while on the back of his neck.

'What do you want?' whined Andvari.

'You want,' said the cavern.

'What I want is all your gold. Otherwise I'll wring you out like a piece of washing. All your gold.'

'All your gold,' boomed the cavern.

Andvari shuddered. He led Loki out of that echoing chamber and down a twisting passage into his smithy. It was hot and smoky but well stocked with gold that gleamed in the firelight. The dwarf spread out his hands and shrugged.

'Gather it up,' said Loki, kicking a gold nugget.

Andvari scrambled around, cursing and moaning. He made a pile of discs and chips and splinters and small bars of red gold, of objects already made and objects half made. Loki looked at the stack and was well satisfied. 'Is that all?' he said.

Andvari said nothing. He stowed the gold into two old sacks; it filled them both. Then, grunting, he dragged them across the smithy and stood with them in front of Loki.

'What about that ring?' said Loki, pointing at the dwarf's closed right hand. 'I saw you hide it.'

Andvari shook his head.

'Put it in the sack,' said Loki.

'Let me keep it,' begged Andvari. 'Just this ring.'

'Put it in the sack,' said Loki.

'Let me keep this, just this,' pleaded the dwarf. 'Then at least I'll be able to make more gold again.'

'I have no need of more,' said Loki, 'and I'm going to strip you to the bone.' He stepped forward and, knocking aside one sack, forced open Andvari's fist and seized the little twisted ring. It was marvellously wrought and Loki slipped it on to his own little finger. 'What is not freely given must be taken by force,' he said.

'Nothing was freely given,' Andvari replied.

Loki shouldered the sacks and turned towards the door of the smithy.

'Take that ring!' yelled the dwarf. 'My curse on that ring and that gold! It will destroy whosoever owns it.'

Loki turned round and faced Andvari. 'So much the better,' he said.

'No one will win joy with my wealth,' shouted Andvari.

'If,' said Loki, 'if I repeat your words to those about to get this gold, then, Andvari, your curse will come to pass.' And with that, Loki turned round again and, with oaths and spells in his ears, made his way out of the world of the dark elves and into Midgard.

'You took your time,' said Odin.

Honir said nothing; he looked rather fearful.

'Hard won and well won,' said Loki. He dumped the sacks of red gold in front of his companions. 'And what do you say to this?' he whispered, showing Odin the twisted ring which he had wrenched from Andvari.

Odin blinked, and marvelled at its subtle beauty. 'Give it to me,' he said.

'At last,' said Hreidmar as he walked into the room, followed by his two sons and two daughters. He nodded, and Fafnir and Regin cut Odin and Honir free from their bonds.

Slowly and stiffly the two gods stood up. They flexed their muscles, they rubbed their hands together, they looked at their chafed wrists and ankles.

'Well, then?' said Hreidmar.

'You must stuff the skin yourself,' said Loki, 'or you'll never be satisfied.' He emptied one sack on to the ground and the magician stowed piece after piece inside Otter's skin. He filled it so that it was plump and taut, bursting from top to tail.

'Now we'll cover it completely,' Loki said, opening the second sack and pouring another mound of metal over the marl floor. While Honir held Otter's skin upright, snout down, Odin and Loki heaped the gold around it. They built Otter a barrow of gold.

'So,' said Odin, with the satisfaction of a job well done, 'come and look for yourself, Hreidmar! We've covered the skin completely.'

The magician walked round and round the stack. He walked round it again. He examined the gold inch by inch. 'Here!' he said. 'Here's a whisker! This must be covered and hidden. Otherwise, I'll hold that you've broken your oath – and that will be the end of our understanding.'

Loki looked at Odin and Odin looked at the twisted ring on his little finger. He sniffed and drew it off and placed it over the single whisker showing. 'Now,' said Odin loudly, 'we've paid Otter's ransom in full.'

'You have indeed,' said Hreidmar.

Still rather unsteady on his feet, Odin lurched across the room to where his spear Gungnir was propped up in the corner. And Loki fell on his sky-shoes and at once put them on. A sense of their own strength surged within them. They looked at Hreidmar and Fafnir and Regin with no great liking.

'Listen carefully!' said Loki. 'That ring and all that gold was made by the dwarf Andvari. I only wrested it from him with his curse.' Loki paused, 'And what he said, I say; what he said will hold.' Loki's voice was low and compelling. 'Take that ring! My curse on that ring and that gold! It will destroy whosoever owns it.'

Odin looked at Loki with his one glittering eye. Loki smiled crookedly. Then Honir took one step and was at their side. The three companions stepped out of the farmhouse into the welcoming spring air.

ALVIS AND THE
RIDDLE CONTEST

THE dwarf Alvis was eager to claim his promised reward for making weapons for the gods. From the world of the dark elves he tramped all the way up to Asgard. Then he hurried towards Thor's hall and in that hall he saw the god he was looking for, but did not recognise him.

'I've come for my bride,' the dwarf said bluntly. 'It's taken long enough to get here, I must say, and now it's high time that Thrud graced her new home. Everyone will say I can't wait for my wedding night, but I don't mean to hang around here any longer than I have to.'

'Who are you?' asked Thor. 'Or should I say, what are you? Why is your nose so pale? Do you sleep in a grave mound and keep corpses company?' Thor considered Alvis. 'You look like a kind of monster. You certainly won't be able to marry Thrud.'

The dwarf drew himself up to his full height, such as it was. 'I am Alvis,' he said, 'and there's nothing I do not know. I live way down under a hill, my home is a cavern hewn out of rock.' Then the dwarf testily brushed aside this talk with a sweep of his hand. 'I've come to claim Thrud – the agreed price for my work and for many weapons. Let the gods not break their oath!'

'I'll break it,' said Thor indignantly. 'I know nothing of this promise.' He stalked down the hall and then called out, 'A father has the last word as to whom his daughter marries. It's up to him and him alone.'

'So who are you, then, hero?' demanded Alvis. 'And what kind of right do you think you have over my radiant bride?' The corners of Alvis's mouth twitched. 'Which woman had to be bought with rings before she would bear you?'

'I,' said the god very slowly, and his eyes flashed so that Alvis began to quail, 'am Thor the Hurler; I am the wide wanderer; and I am Odin's son. You'll never win and marry my daughter if I can help it.'

'Ah!' said Alvis, his mouth dropped open. 'Well, I'll soon win your good will and your consent. I long for your snow-white daughter and I'll struggle for her.'

'Wise guest,' said Thor, 'I won't be able to stand in the way of your love if you can answer whatever I ask you about all the worlds. Tell me, Alvis! You're the dwarf who knows everything about our fates and fortunes: what is the name for the land, that stretches all around us, in each and every world?'

'Men call it Earth,' the dwarf replied. 'The Aesir say Field and the Vanir say the Ways. The giants name it Evergreen and the elves Grower. The most holy gods call it Clay.'

'Tell me, Alvis! You're the dwarf who knows everything about our fates and fortunes: what is the name for the sky, child of the ocean, that we can all see, in each and every world?'

'Men call it Heaven,' the dwarf replied. 'The gods say the Height and the Vanir say Wind Weaver. The giants name it High Home, the elves Fair Roof and the dwarfs Dripping Hall.'

'Tell me, Alvis! You're the dwarf who knows everything about our fates and fortunes: what is the name for the moon, that we can all see, in each and every world?'

'Men call it Moon.' the dwarf replied, 'but the gods say Mock Sun. It's known in Hel as Whirling Wheel. The giants name it Rapid Traveller, the dwarfs Gleamer and the elves Time Teller.'

'Tell me, Alvis! You're the dwarf who knows everything about our fates and fortunes: what is the name for the sun, that we can all see, in each and every world?'

'Men call it Sun,' the dwarf replied. 'The gods say Orb and the dwarfs Dvalin's Delight. The giants name it Ever Bright, the elves Fair Wheel and the sons of god All Glowing.'

'Tell me, Alvis! You're the dwarf who knows everything about our fates and fortunes: what is the name for the clouds, that hold the rain, in each and every world?'

'Men call them Clouds,' the dwarf replied. 'The gods say Chance of Showers and the Vanir say Wind Kites. The giants name them Hope of Rain, the elves Weather Might, and in Hel they're known as Helmets of Secrets.'

'Tell me, Alvis! You're the dwarf who knows everything about our fates and fortunes: what is the name for the wind, that ranges far and wide, in each and every world?'

'Men call it Wind,' the dwarf replied. 'The gods say Waverer and the most holy gods call it Neigher. The giants name it Wailer, the elves Roaring Traveller, and in Hel it's known as Blustering Blast.'

'Tell me, Alvis! You're the dwarf who knows everything about our fates and fortunes: what is the name for the stillness, the settling peace, in each and every world?'

'Men call it Calm,' the dwarf replied. 'The gods say the Quiet and the Vanir say Winds' Hush. The giants name it the Sultry, the elves Day's Lull and the dwarfs Day's Refuge.'

'Tell me, Alvis! You're the dwarf who knows everything about our fates and fortunes: what is the name for the sea, on which men sail, in each and every world?'

'Men call it Sea,' the dwarf replied. 'The gods say Smooth-lying and the Vanir say Waves. The giants name it Eel Home, the elves Drink Stuff and the dwarfs call it the Deep.'

'Tell me, Alvis! You're the dwarf who knows everything about our fates and fortunes: what is the name for fire, that burns for men, in each and every world?'

'Men call it Fire,' the dwarf replied. 'The gods say Flame and the Vanir say Wave. The giants name it Hungry Biter, and the dwarfs Burner. In Hel it's known as the Hasty.'

'Tell me, Alvis! You're the dwarf who knows everything about our fates and fortunes: what is the name for the wood, that grows for men, in each and every world?'

'Men call it Wood,' the dwarf replied. 'The gods say Mane of the Field and in Hel it's knows as Seaweed of the Hills. The giants name it Fuel and the elves Fair-limbed. The Vanir call it Wand.'

'Tell me, Alvis! You're the dwarf who knows everything about our fates and fortunes: what is the name for the night, daughter of Narvi, in each and every world?'

'Men call it Night,' the dwarf replied. 'The gods say Darkness and the most holy gods say Hood. The giants name it Lightless, the elves Sleep's Soothing and the dwarfs the Weaver of Dreams.'

'Tell me, Alvis! You're the dwarf who knows everything about our fates and fortunes: what is the name for the seed, sown by men, in each and every world?'

'Men call it Barley,' the dwarf replied. 'The gods say Grain and the Vanir say Growth. The giants name it Edible, the elves Drink Grist, and in Hel it's known as Slender Stem.'

'Tell me, Alvis! You're the dwarf who knows everything about our fates and fortunes: what is the name for ale, that men quaff, in each and every world?'

'Men call it Ale,' the dwarf replied. 'The gods say Beer and the Vanir say Foaming. The giants name it Cloudless Swill, and in Hel it's known as Mead. The giant Suttung's sons call it Fast Draught.'

Thor said, 'I've never known one person to be the mine of so much ancient wisdom.' He smiled at his guest, a long slow smile, and he slowly nodded his head. 'But your own tongue has trapped you, Alvis. The sun's rays arrest you.'

The dwarf whirled round but it was already too late.

'The sun's rays arrest you,' gloated Thor, 'and they turn you into stone. And now the sun shines in my hall once again.'

BALDER'S DREAMS

THE god moaned. He twisted and writhed as he tried to escape the dark shapes. He panted and moaned again, and then he woke. For a long while the fairest of the gods lay in the half light, his brow gleaming as white as the whitest flower, his hair shining, and he tried to snare his dream – to name each form and dismiss it. But the shapes skulked in the shadows, shapeless now that he was awake. And in time his fear lapsed into a dull foreboding; he closed his eyes and began to drift.

No sooner was he asleep than his ghastly skull-guests crept forward yet again, monstrous forms intent on snuffing out the light of him. He threshed and kicked. He called out and his own shout woke him. Once more he felt fearful and exposed and doomed.

When the gods and goddesses heard about Balder's dreams they anxiously gathered to discuss their meaning. They said that he was the most merciful, the most gentle and loved of them all, the least deserving of such unwelcome night visitors; they said nothing tainted had ever crossed the threshold of his hall before. But all they said only disturbed them more. They could not unravel Balder's dreams.

'I will go myself,' said Odin, Balder's father, 'and return with a meaning.' The one-eyed god, old as time, stood up and hurried out

of the council. He saddled Sleipnir, galloped over the quivering
rainbow, and took the long, long track that led north from Midgard
down into the gloom and the swirling mists of Niflheim.

Hel's hound heard Odin coming. The hair on Garm's throat and
chest was caked with blood and he bayed from his cliff cave at the
entrance to the underworld. Odin took no notice. He galloped so
hard that the frozen ground thrummed under Sleipnir's eight
hooves, and he did not let up until he had reached Hel's forbidding
hall.

Here Odin dismounted. He peered into the hall – it was packed
out with the dead, and gleaming with gold rings and gold ornaments; then he led Sleipnir round to the east door near which a
seeress was buried. Odin stood beside her mound and fixed his one
glittering eye upon it. Then he began to use charms and, in the
gloom, the pale spectre of the seeress rose out of the earth and
loomed over him.

'Who,' she moaned, 'who is the stranger who forces me up and
unearths me to sorrows? Snow has settled on me, rain has lashed
me, dew has seeped through me; I have long been dead.'

'My name is Wanderer,' Odin said. 'Give me news of Hel; I have
travelled already through the other worlds. Why are gold rings
strewn along the benches in Hel's hall and why is the whole place
decorated with gold? Who are you expecting?'

'The shining mead,' said the seeress, 'is brewed for Balder; a shield covers the cauldron. For all their glory, the gods will be filled with despair. I was unwilling to speak and I will say no more now.'

'Seeress, you must stay,' said Odin. 'You must answer all that I ask. Who will slay Balder and drain the life-blood of Odin's son?'

'His brother blind Hod will carry a fatal branch. He will slay Balder and drain the life-blood of Odin's son. I was unwilling to speak and I will say no more now.'

'Seeress, you must stay,' Odin said. 'You must answer all that I ask. Who will take vengeance on Hod? Who will carry Balder's slayer to the pyre?'

'The goddess Rind will lie with Odin,' said the seeress, 'and their son will be Vali. He will take vengeance when he is only one night old. He will not wash his hands nor comb his hair before he has carried Balder's slayer to the pyre. I was unwilling to speak and I will say no more now.'

'Seeress, you must stay,' Odin said. 'You must answer all that I ask. Who are the maidens who will keen then, and toss their scarves up against the sky?'

'You are not Wanderer,' said the seeress, 'as I believed you to be. You are Odin, the magician, old as time.'

'And you are no seeress,' Odin said, 'nor are you wise. You are the mother of three monsters.'

'Ride home, Odin, and boast about your skills,' said the seeress. Her voice was rising and gloating. 'No one will raise me again until Loki breaks free from his fetters and all the forces of darkness gather before Ragnarok.'

The spectre, pale and gleaming, began to ooze and to sink back into her grave.

Then Odin turned away. He mounted Sleipnir with a heavy heart.

THE DEATH
OF BALDER

THE gods and goddesses gathered in the shadow of Balder's terrible dreams, dreams that threatened to pitch him into the darkness for ever. Not one of them doubted his life was in danger and for a long time they discussed how to protect him.

The gods and goddesses thought of all the ways in which one can die; they named each earth-thing, sea-thing and sky-thing that can cause sudden death. Then Balder's mother, Frigg, began to travel through the nine worlds and get each and every substance to swear an oath that it would not harm Balder.

Fire swore an oath. Water swore an oath. Iron and every other kind of metal swore an oath. The stones swore oaths. Nothing could stay Frigg from her mission or resist her sweet troubled persuasion. Earth swore an oath. The trees swore oaths. Each kind of illness swore an oath. Balder's mother was untiring and painstaking. All the animals swore an oath and so did every sidling snake.

Then the gods and goddesses met again and Frigg satisfied them that she had done as they asked, and that nothing in creation would harm Balder.

'We should put it to the test,' they said. And one picked up a pebble and lobbed it so that it landed right on Balder's head.

Whatever power that small stone had, it withheld it. Balder did not even know that the pebble had struck him. 'I could not feel it at all,' he said.

Then all the gods and goddesses laughed. They left Gladsheim and streamed out into the sunlight. The hall's gold roof and gold walls were glowing and the green plain surrounding it teemed with activity – the gods' servants coming and going, troops of light elves hurrying about their business, visitors to Asgard staring in wonder about them, and animals of many kinds grazing or dozing, all of them glad to be alive.

*   *   *

The foremost gods met in Gladsheim and the goddesses in Vingolf. They ruled over Asgard; they discussed the feats and the fates of heroic men in Midgard. And after their councils, they often met together and were joined by a jostling throng – gossiping, sociable, eager for amusement. Sometimes they drank, sometimes they sang, they made trials of their strength and played games of all kinds.

It was not long before the gods thought they should check Balder's safety again; they could not resist the sport. One tossed a pebble at him and it struck him on the cheekbone; another aimed a stick at him and hit him on the chest.

'I could not feel them at all,' said Balder.

Then the gods laughed and tried other tests. One thing led to another and soon they became very bold. They made Balder stand against a wall as a target. Some threw darts with wicked points at him, and the darts bounced off him and fell at his feet. Some brought in stones and hurled them at him. The rest struck at him with axes and slashed at him with swords and the tempered metal would not scathe Balder, it would not even graze him. The fairest and most gentle of the gods became the butt of the most violent assaults and they did not harm him. Everyone present enjoyed this new game hugely and they all rejoiced that it was impossible to hurt him.

All except Loki: the Sly One watched with distaste and impatience. Trouble and suffering were meat and drink to him, and it sickened him to see that Balder was immune from every kind of attack. This grudge grew in him day by day and began to consume him. He refused to take part in the games and yet he was unable to keep away.

One afternoon Loki was loafing as usual against the door of Gladsheim, watching the assembly, when an idea occurred to him. He half closed his eyes; he licked his twisted lips and smiled. Unnoticed, he stepped out of the hubbub and quickly walked off in the direction of Frigg's hall.

Loki paused. He had a careful look round; there was nobody about. Then he whispered the charm; the Shape Changer turned himself into an old woman.

As Loki hoped, Frigg was in her hall and alone. The old woman hobbled across the floor; she sniffed, wiped her dripping nose with the back of her hand and rubbed it against her grubby dark dress. 'Where am I?' she demanded.

Frigg rose, greeted the old woman, and named herself.

'It's a long way from home,' observed the old woman. 'And I'm not sure it's been worth coming.'

Frigg listened patiently.

'I passed a place some way back. What a noise! I couldn't get anyone to listen. And the people there were all stoning one man. Poor man! He had a white face, so white . . . shining hair. One against all, yes; I didn't know that sort of thing went on in Asgard.'

Frigg smiled faintly and thought it wise to wait until the old woman had had her say.

'I didn't stay long; I never did like stonings. Who would have thought it? So far to have come, and then it's much the same. He'll be dead by now, yes.' As the old woman rambled on, it seemed she had quite forgotten she was in company. But now she shook her head fiercely and glared at Frigg. 'What was going on then? Do you know why they are stoning him?'

Frigg told the old woman that what she had seen was not a stoning but a host of gods and goddesses sporting with her own son. She explained that Balder had not been hurt by a single stone and was just as ready to take part as anyone else.

'What kind of magic is that then?' asked the old woman. She had the makings of a moustache and it was twitching in rather a disturbing way.

'Nothing will hurt Balder,' replied Frigg. 'No metal will harm him, no wood will wound him. I've taken an oath from everything.'

'Everything?' said the old woman. 'Even a pinch of salt, I suppose?'

Frigg began to feel irritated with this wearisome crone; she shrugged as if she were trying to get rid of her.

'Everything?' The old woman sniffed. 'Everything has sworn an oath it will not injure Balder?'

'Everything,' said Frigg dismissively, 'except the little bush that grows west of Valhalla, the mistletoe. That's so young I didn't bother with it.'

The old woman grunted. 'Well you've given me the time of day,' she said. 'You've given me the time of day, yes; now I'll be getting along.'

Frigg inclined her head.

The old woman turned and painfully made her way to the doors of the hall. And Frigg was not in the least sorry to see her go.

As soon as he was quite certain he was alone, the Shape Changer muttered the magic words. Then, crowing, he resumed his old form: Loki again.

Jauntily the Trickster walked across the great plain – deserted now except for the animals that stood in motionless groups, as if they were waiting, or had never moved. The air was thickening, the distance and middle distance were blurred and bluish; it was almost night.

Loki hurried past Gladsheim. He hurried towards Valhalla and smiled to himself as he heard the warriors shouting. He hurried on west in the fading light, whistling and looking sharply to left and right and under his feet. Then he entered a small grove. And there, rooted neither in earth nor water, but growing out of the trunk of an oak, the Sly One found what he had come for – the spray of mistletoe.

Its berries gleamed like clusters of pale eyes. Its leaves were green and yellow-green, its stem and small branches and twigs were green. Unmoving and otherworldly it seemed in broad daylight, and even more strange now in the half light.

Loki grabbed at the little bush and wrenched at it until it came away from the oak. Then he left the grove and took the path to Gladsheim, picking at the spray as he hurried along. He chose the straightest branch, almost as long as his forearm, and stripped it down, leaving a small trail of droppings behind him. Loki sharpened one end of it; he stropped it against his belt, and stepped into the warm light of the hall.

The gathering in Gladsheim was so caught up in the game they were playing that no one was aware Loki had gone and no one noticed he had come back again. The Sly One looked around. He smiled when he saw that Frigg had joined the company; his lips tightened and his eyes narrowed as he watched blind Hod, Balder's brother, standing a little aside as usual – pathetic in his slow fumbling movements; and when Loki saw that many of the gods were once again hurling darts at long-suffering Balder, he doubled up. For a moment his whole body was convulsed, as if in laughter or terrible pain.

A servant hurried up and offered Loki wine. Loki drained the cup at one draught and then sauntered across the spacious hall, behind the semicircle of the gods and their followers. He sidled up to Hod and poked him in the ribs.

'That can only be Loki,' said Hod.

'None other,' said a voice in his ear.

'Well?' said Hod.

'Why don't you join in? Why aren't you throwing darts at your brother?'

'Because I can't see where he is,' said Hod.

Loki sucked his cheeks.

'Another thing,' said Hod. 'I have no weapon.'

'This is not as it should be,' said Loki with measured indignation. 'They do wrong to ignore you – and you his brother.'

Hod's expression did not alter. He had long since learned to accept his fate. 'Nothing comes,' he said, 'of rankling resentment.'

Hod's words were drowned in a roar of laughter.

'What was that?' he asked.

'Only more of the same,' said Loki. 'A dart well aimed. But now it's your turn, Hod. You should pay your respects to Balder like everybody else.'

'I have no weapon,' Hod repeated.

'Take this twig then,' said Loki, and he placed the sharpened mistletoe between Hod's hands. 'I'll show you where he's standing. I'll stand behind you and guide your hand.'

Loki's eyes were on fire now. His whole body was on fire. His face was ravaged by wolfish evil and hunger.

Hod grasped the mistletoe and lifted his right arm. Guided by Loki, he aimed the dart at his brother Balder.

The mistletoe flew through the hall and it struck Balder. It pierced him and passed right through him. The god fell on his face. He was dead.

There was no sound in Gladsheim, no sound, only the roaring of silence. The gods could not speak. They looked at the fairest and most wise of them all, shining and lifeless, and they could not even move from where they stood to lift him.

The gods stared at each other and then they turned to stare at Hod and Loki. They had no doubt. They were all of one mind about who had caused Balder's death and yet none of them were able to take vengeance. The ground of Gladsheim was hallowed and no one was ready to shed blood in the sanctuary.

Hod could not see the fearsome gaze of that gathering; Loki could not withstand it. He loped towards the doors of Gladsheim and slunk away into the darkness.

Then the terrible silence was broken. One goddess began to weep, seized by wild grief. And the weeping of one unlocked the floodgates of them all. When they tried to speak, they found they could not tell their grief and their words were choked with tears.

Odin himself was there and, of all the gods and goddesses, he was the most deeply afflicted. He best understood that this was the greatest evil ever sustained by gods and men, and foresaw what loss and sorrow would follow in the wake of his son's death.

Frigg was the first to speak. 'Does anyone . . .' she asked. 'Does anyone here want to win all my love and favour?'

The mourning company turned to face her.

'Is there anyone here who will ride the long road to Hel and try to find Balder?'

Then the goddesses buried their faces in their hands and sobbed again.

'Is there anyone here,' said Frigg, her voice rising, 'who will offer Hel a ransom, offer her a ransom if she'll allow my son to come home to Asgard again?'

Then Hermod stepped forward, Odin's son whom everyone admired for his boldness. 'I will,' he said, 'I am ready to go.'

Gladsheim began to breathe and sound again. Odin gave servants orders. They hurried out of the hall and soon returned with Sleipnir, Odin's own horse.

Allfather took the reins and handed them to Hermod, and Hermod mounted. He looked down at the upturned faces of the gods and goddesses and at the fair fallen body of Balder. He raised his hand and spurred his steed; Sleipnir's hooves clattered against the marble floor. Hermod galloped out into the darkness and on towards the endless night.

The gods and goddesses did not sleep; they kept a silent vigil in Gladsheim. Ranged around Balder's body, so white that it was gleaming, each of them was prey to his own thoughts and hopes and fears – what chance Hermod had of bringing Balder back from the dead, how to avenge Balder's death on his own unhappy brother Hod, what kind of punishment would begin to suffice for Loki, and what meaning the death of one must have for them all.

Day began to dawn: a lightening in the east at first mysterious, then quickly gathering speed and spreading in every direction.

Then with aching hearts, four of the gods lifted Balder's body on to their shoulders, and all the others formed a long cortège. They carried him down to the sea and laid his corpse near Ringhorn, his own great boat with its curved prow.

The gods wanted to build Balder's pyre in the waist of the boat, up against the mast. They took hold of the stern and tried to launch the boat, but their grief had so exhausted them that they could not summon up the strength to shift it on its rollers.

Then the gods sent a messenger speeding to Jotunheim to ask for the help of the giantess Hyrrokin. A great crowd out of Asgard sat near the water, watching the pulse of the waves. They were pensive and subdued, none of them so strong that he could escape the flux of his own feelings and comfort the others.

In a while Hyrrokin came. She was huge and grim, riding a wolf with vipers for reins. As soon as she leaped off her steed, Odin summoned four Berserks and told them to watch over the wolf (and the vipers) and ensure they caused no harm.

The very sight of the four men in their animal skins angered the wolf; its eyes flickered and it snarled.

The Berserks seized the viper-reins but they were unable to hold the wolf fast. First it dragged them one way, then another, slithering helplessly through the sand, as it tried to break free. Then the Berserks became as mad as wolves themselves and in fury they rained blows on the wolf with their club-like fists. They struck it down and left it for dead in the sand.

Hyrrokin, meanwhile, stalked up to Ringhorn. She looked at the boat, so large and yet so sweeping and graceful, and gripped the prow. Then she dug in her heels and with a horrible grunt she pulled – pulled so hard that Ringhorn raced screaming down the rollers and crashed into the water. The pine rollers burst into flames and the nine worlds trembled.

'Enough!' shouted Thor. His fingers closed round his hammer and he felt his old strength surging back into him.

Hyrrokin looked at Thor scornfully.

'Enough!' repeated Thor. 'I'll teach you respect.'

But Odin and several other gods hurried to Thor's side and restrained him. They took his arm and reminded him, 'She is here at our bidding.'

'I'll crack her skull,' muttered Thor.

'It would be wrong to injure her,' said the gods. 'Leave her. Ignore her.'

And slowly Thor's volcanic anger subsided inside him. He kicked at the sand, causing a sandstorm, and walked up and down.

Then the four gods who had carried Balder's body down to the sea gently raised it again and waded out to Ringhorn, rocking on the water. They set down his spotless body on a high bench, covered in crimson cloth.

Balder's wife, Nanna, was watching. And when she saw Balder lying there lifeless, her body shook; she could not control it. She was tearless, in too much pain for tears now. Then her heart broke. Nanna died there, and she was carried out to Ringhorn and laid beside her dead husband.

The cortège had swollen to a vast gathering. Odin was there; his ravens, Thought and Memory, perched on his shoulders. Frigg accompanied him, and so did the Valkyries: Shaker and Mist, Axe Time and Raging, Warrior and Might, Shrieking, Host Fetter and Screaming, Spear Bearer, Shield Bearer, Wrecker of Plans – all those beautiful maidens, choosers of the slain, stood grouped around the Father of Battle.

Freyr had come to the cremation in his chariot drawn by Gullinbursti, the gold-bristled boar fashioned for him by the dwarfs. Heimdall had come on his mount Gold Tuft. And Freyja sat in her chariot drawn by cats.

The elves were there. The dwarfs were there. And hundreds of frost giants and rock giants stood there too, a great gang who had followed Hyrrokin out of Jotunheim. That was a vast concourse, a mingling of mourners and the merely curious on the foreshore, scuffing the strip of sand that never wholly belongs to earth or to sea. The seabirds rose and wheeled and dipped, screaming, the sea sobbed, and everyone there watched the ritual on Ringhorn.

A pyre was built round the body of Balder and his wife Nanna, dry faggots that needed nothing more than a spark to leap into their own life and consume the lifeless bodies that lay upon them, releasing their spirits to travel on.

Then many treasures were laid within Ringhorn – buckles and brooches and rings, clasps and pins – and not only treasures but knives and buckets and scissors and spindles and spades and all the fabric of life.

Balder's horse, meanwhile, was galloping along the foreshore and worked into a streaming sweat. Then a servant plunged a short dagger into its throat. It gave a violent jerk and, without a sound, crumpled amongst the wrack. No sooner was it dead than its body was hacked up, and the pieces were thrown into Ringhorn.

Now Odin strode through the shallows and gripped the gunwale. He climbed into the boat and stood over the body of his dead son. For some time he gazed at him. Slowly he took off his arm-ring Draupnir, the gold ring that dropped eight rings of equal value on every ninth night, and slipped it on to Balder's arm. Then Odin bent down and put his mouth to Balder's ear. Again he gazed at his son; then he left Ringhorn.

At a sign from Odin a servant stepped forward with a lighted brand. He set fire to the pyre and at once a steady plume of smoke, twisting and spiralling, rose into the calm air.

Thor slowly raised his hammer. Slowly and solemnly he intoned the magic words to hallow the cremation.

Then a dwarf called Lit, who had lost all interest in the proceedings, came running along the water's edge. He passed right in front of Thor and Thor was so enraged that he put out a foot and tripped him. Before Lit had time to pick himself up, Thor gave him a terrible kick. The dwarf flew through the air and landed right on the licking and curdling pyre. In this way, he was burned to death beside Balder.

The painter was released and with it the pent emotions of the mourners. They wept as the boat began to drift out, rocking, across the water. They wept and they talked about Balder – the most beautiful, the most gentle, the most wise of them all.

Ringhorn rode across the water. Sea winds caught at her and tugged her away. First she was more boat than flame, but soon more flame than boat. She was a quivering shape, a farewell on the horizon, moving on under a great cloud of her own making.

For nine nights Hermod rode through a valley so deep and dark that he was unable to see anything. The ground fell away from him and the cold fingers of the underworld began to reach up towards him and search him. The god crossed eleven rivers, all of which spring from the seething cauldron of Hvergelmir, and the last of them was the icy river Gjoll, a swirling torrent of water. Sleipnir needed no spurring. He galloped across the bridge there; it was thatched with strips of gold.

On the far side, Hermod was stopped by the maiden who was warden of the bridge. She raised one pale arm and it gleamed with an unearthly pallor. 'Before you go further,' she said, 'tell me your name and your lineage.'

Hermod kept quiet.

'Five troops of dead men came this way yesterday,' said the warden. 'They rode over this bridge. But you make as much noise as they all made together.'

Still Hermod said nothing.

'I can't say you look like a man who has died,' said the maiden. 'Who are you?'

'I am Hermod,' said the god, 'and I am Odin's son. I must ride to Hel in search of my dead brother. Have you seen him yourself on his way there?'

'He has crossed this river,' the maiden replied. 'He rode over this bridge. But the way to Hel is no short way; far as you have come, it is still a little further northwards and downwards.'

Hermod thanked the maiden and she stepped aside. Then Sleipnir saw the way before him: horse and rider galloped onward. So at last Hermod came to the massive gates and towering walls that Hel had set up in front of her hall.

Sleipnir stopped in his tracks and whinnied.

Hermod dismounted and looked around in the dismal light. The gates were locked; impassable, it seemed, for all those not fated to pass beyond on their way to dreadful Nastrond, the shore of corpses. Hermod tightened his stirrups. He swung himself into the saddle and spurred Sleipnir fiercely.

Odin's steed galloped at the gates. For a moment he seemed to pause, then he gave a great thrust with his back legs and leaped clear of the iron gates.

Hermod boldly took Sleipnir right up to the hall doors. There he dismounted once more and walked straight into the cavernous hall. Faces without number turned towards him – the faces of the newly dead, faces green and rotting, faces less flesh and bone; faces pitiful, unanswered, resigned, many scowling or leering or treacherous or murderous and in agony, all of them with eyes only for Hermod.

But Hermod saw only the fair figure sitting in the high seat: his brother Balder.

For Balder's sake and the sake of the gods, resolute Hermod stayed all night in the hall. He sat by the door and kept his own counsel, silent in that company of the dead who could not speak unless he spoke to them; he waited for Hel to rise from Sick Bed and draw back its hangings, Glimmering Misfortune.

Hel's face and body were those of a living woman, but her thighs and legs were those of a corpse, mottled and mouldering. She crept towards the god, looking gloomy and grim.

Hermod greeted Hel and told her of the grief of the gods. He said all Asgard was caught in a tearfall and a storm of sorrow. He wove his words with care and love and asked Hel if she would agree to let Balder ride home with him.

Hel thought for a while and her expression did not change. 'I'm not so sure,' she said at last, 'that Balder is as much loved as people say.'

She waited for Hermod to reply and Hermod said nothing.

'However,' said Hel, 'it can be put to the test.' She spoke as slowly as her aged servants moved – so slowly that her words were only punctuations between her silences. 'If everything in the nine worlds, dead and alive, weeps for Balder,' Hel declared, 'let him return to Asgard. But if anything demurs, if even one thing will not weep, Balder must remain in Niflheim.' And with these words Hel slowly turned away.

Then Balder stood up and Nanna rose from the shades and stood beside him. They walked the length of the hall; they passed between the benches of corpses and Balder's face was white and shining. Balder and Nanna came up to Hermod and greeted him and led him out of the hall. Then Balder took off the arm-ring that Odin had fixed on him when he was lying lifeless on Ringhorn, and he put it into Hermod's hands. He said, 'Give this to my father in remembrance of me.' And Nanna offered Hermod linen for a head-dress and other gifts. 'These are for Frigg,' she said. 'And this is for her maid-servant.' She handed Hermod a gold ring.

Hermod took leave of Balder and Nanna. He rode without rest until he reached Asgard. And there, in Gladsheim, he told the gods gods and goddesses all he had seen and all that had been said to him.

The Aesir sent out messengers to every corner of the nine worlds. And all that they asked was that dead Balder should be wept out of Hel. As each substance had sworn an oath before that it would not harm Balder, each substance now wept. Fire wept, iron and every other metal wept, the stones wept, earth wept, the trees wept, every kind of illness wept, all the animals wept, all the birds wept, every kind of poisonous plant wept and so did every sidling snake – just as these things weep when they are covered with rime and begin to thaw again.

The gods' messengers were making their way back to Asgard and they all felt they had overlooked nothing. Then they came across a giantess sitting in a cave.

'What is your name?' asked one.

'Thokk,' said the giantess.

Then the messengers explained their mission and asked Thokk to weep as all things had wept, weep and weep Balder out of Hel.

The giantess glowered at the messengers and then she answered sourly, 'Thokk will weep dry tears over Balder's funeral. I never cared for the Old Man's son – alive or dead, I have no use for him. Let Hel hold what she has.'

Despite the messengers' prayers and entreaties, Thokk refused to say another word. She would not recant, she would not weep.

Then the messengers left her; they mournfully crossed Bifrost. And what they had to say was clear from the manner of their coming.

The gods and goddesses ached; they felt old and confused and unable and weary. And not one of them doubted that Thokk, the giantess in the cave, was also Loki.

THE BINDING OF
LOKI

LOKI knew that his days in Asgard had come to an end. He knew
how soon anguish can give way to anger and was sure the gods
would avenge Balder's death and detention in Hel.

He ran away. He made for a deserted part of Midgard, a remote
place in the mountains at the head of a steep valley that fell into the
sea. He found a hollow near Franang's Falls and, using the rock and
rubble lying all around, built a low house that no man was likely to
see until he had stumbled into it. It had four doors so that Loki
could keep watch in every direction.

Even so, he felt unsafe. When a gull circled and shrieked, or scree
shifted on the mountain, or wind whistled in his walls, the Trickster
leaped up in alarm, certain he had been tracked down. It did not
matter that days passed without a single visitor: Loki's anxiety grew
greater day by day; he could not escape his own canker.

He thought he might be better off if he were out of the house and
in disguise. At dawn the Shape Changer often turned himself into a
salmon and leaped into the seething cauldron at the base of Franang's Falls. The cross currents whirled around him, the thunder
roared above him; still the salmon felt unsafe.

In Loki's mind it was not a question of whether the gods would
catch up with him, but of when. But fearful as he was, hunted and
in hiding, he was more fearful of vengeance, and vowed to remain
at large as long as he had the wits to do so.

Early one evening, Loki sat beside his fire and began to play with
some lengths of linen twine. He arranged them and rearranged them;
he laid them out across each other and tied them and made them
into a net with so fine a mesh that not even a small fish could hope
to slip through it. For a long time he stared at his fine device.

Suddenly he heard the sound of voices down in the valley; he saw
a group of gods making their way towards him. Loki jumped up,
threw the net into the fire and hurried out of the door overlooking
Franang's Falls. He ran down the slope, turned himself into a salmon
once more and slid into the boiling icy water.

*   *   *

There was nothing that escaped Odin's eye when he sat in Hlidskjalf. He saw the comings and goings of every living creature in the nine worlds; and when he saw Loki's efforts to escape his fate, he sent a party of gods from Asgard to capture him.

The first to step across the threshold of Loki's house was Kvasir, the wisest of them all. In the half light, he peered around without a word. He looked at the rough table and bench, the bare walls, the almost lifeless fire. Kvasir bent down and stared at the pattern of gleaming white ash; he carefully examined it and understood what he saw. 'This,' he said to his companions, 'is some device for catching fish. Let us catch a fish.'

The gods sat down in Loki's house and gave over the rest of the evening to making a wide net with which to drag the pool at the base of the Falls and the river that hurried down the valley to the sea. They copied the subtle pattern Kvasir had found in the embers and, before they slept, they had finished their work and were well content with it.

At dawn the gods walked down under Franang's Falls. The roar of water slamming against water was deafening. The air was misty with whirling and drifting spray; the gods stared around them and the whole world looked oyster and ivory and grey. Then Thor took one end of the net and, motioning to the others to stay where they were, waded across the water. So the gods began to drag the river and the salmon swam downstream in front of them. After a time, wily Loki found a safe place where the water sluiced between two slimy boulders and he nestled there so that the net only scraped his back and did not snare him. When the gods brought up the net, there was nothing in it. They were all sure, though, that they had felt something alive in the water. They decided to try again, and this time to use stones to weight the bottom of the drag-net so that nothing could swim under it.

Now, the gods made their way back to the base of Franang's Falls – Thor on one side and all the rest on the other – and dropped the net into the water. Once more Loki swam ahead of them as they dragged the river, but this time there was no safety on the river bed. He had no choice but to hurry on downstream. When Loki saw that the gods meant to drag the tumbling river right down to the shallows where it opened on to the sea, he turned round to face the net. He arched his back, and with all his strength, sprang into the air and right over it.

The gods shouted and pointed at the salmon shining in the sunlight. They hurried back up to Franang's Falls and there they argued
about how to catch it. Each god had his own idea but, in the end,
they bowed to Kvasir: he said they should split into two groups –
one on either bank – all except Thor who was to wade in midstream
just behind the net.

Now the gods began to drag the river for a third time. As before,
Loki swam downstream some way in front of them. He knew that
only two choices were open to him: to squirm and jump across the
long stretch of shallows into the sea or to turn and leap over the
drag-net again. He thought the gods might catch him before he
reached the safety of deep water and so he turned, arched his back
into a rainbow, and sprang into the air. The salmon flashed in the
sunlight and jumped clear of the net.

Then Thor groped and clutched at it and the salmon slithered through his hands. Thor held on and tightened his grip; he squeezed and stayed the slippery salmon by its tail. It writhed and it twisted but it could not escape. Loki was caught at last and he knew it.

After Balder's death, not one of the gods would stain Gladsheim by spilling Loki's blood. But there was nothing holy about the barren ground of Midgard, and they were all eager to take vengeance on him.

While Thor and one group of gods led Loki into a twilit cave, a dismal cavern belonging to bats and ticking with the drips of water from stalactites, the other party went off in pursuit of Loki's two sons, Vali and Narvi. They changed Vali into a wolf and at once he leaped at his brother and sunk his teeth into his throat. He ripped Narvi's body apart before bounding away, howling, toward Jotunheim.

The gods took over where Vali had left off. They drew out Narvi's entrails and made their way to the cave. Loki's faithful wife, Sigyn, went with them, sorrowing over the fate of her two sons, the fate of her husband.

Loki was thrown to the ground. He lay still; he looked at nobody and said nothing. Then the gods took three slabs of rock, stood them on end and bored a hole through each of them. They stretched Loki over them, unwound Narvi's entrails and bound him with the gut of his own son as no one had ever been bound before. They trussed Loki's shoulders to one slab, twisting the gut round his body under his armpits; they strapped Loki's loins to one slab, winding the gut round and round his hips; they clamped Loki's kneecaps to one slab, tying the gut round his legs. And no sooner was Loki bound than the entrails of his son became as hard as iron.

Then the gods carried a vile snake into the cave, and fastened it to a stalactite high up in the darkness so that its venom would drip straight on to Loki's face. For all his wiles and wit, there was nothing Loki could do. He lay still; he looked at nobody and said nothing. Then the gods left Loki there; no longer flushed but heavy-hearted and sorrowing they left him to his fate, and to faithful Sigyn.

Sigyn and Loki wait in the damp twilit cave, listening to the eerie echoes of each drip, the sound of the silence, the sound of their own breathing. Sigyn holds a wooden bowl over Loki's face and slowly it fills with the snake's venom. When it is brimming, Sigyn carries the bowl away and empties it into a rock basin – a fermenting pool of poison.

Loki is left unguarded; he screws up his eyes. The snake does not wait. Its venom splashes on to Loki's face and in torment he shudders and writhes. He cannot escape and the whole earth quakes.

Loki lies bound. That is how things are and how things will remain until Ragnarok.

RAGNAROK

AN axe-age, a sword-age, shields will be gashed: there will be a wind-age and a wolf-age before the world is wrecked.

First of all Midgard will be wrenched and racked by wars for three winters. Fathers will slaughter sons; brothers will be drenched in one another's blood. Mothers will desert their menfolk and seduce their own sons; brothers will bed with sisters.

Then Fimbulvetr, the winter of winters, will grip and throttle Midgard. Driving snow clouds will converge from north and south and east and west. There will be bitter frosts, biting winds; the shining sun will be helpless. Three such winters will follow each other with no summers between them.

So the end will begin. Then the children of the old giantess in Iron Wood will have their say: the wolf Skoll will seize the sun between his jaws and swallow her – he will spatter Asgard with gore; and his brother Hati will catch the moon and mangle him. The stars will vanish from the sky.

The earth will start to shudder then. Great trees will sway and topple, mountains will shake and rock and come crashing down, and every bond and fetter will burst. Fenrir will run free.

The watchman of the giants will sit on his grave mound and strum his harp, smiling grimly. Nothing escapes the red cock Fjalar; he will crow to the giants from bird-wood. At the same time the cock who wakes the warriors every day in Valhalla will crow to the gods. A third cock, rust red, will raise the dead in Hel.

The sea will rear up and waves will pummel the shore because the Midgard Serpent is twisting and writhing in fury, working his way on to dry land. And in those high seas a great boat will break loose – a ship made from dead men's nails. The bows and the waist and the stern and the hold will be packed with giants heading towards the plain Vigrid. Loki too, free from his fetters, will take to the water; he will set sail towards Vigrid from the north and his deadweight will be all that ghastly crew in Hel.

Then the brothers Fenrir and Jormungand will move forward side by side. Fenrir's slavering mouth will gape wide open, so wide that his lower jaw scrapes against the ground and his upper jaw presses against the sky; it would gape still wider if there were more room. Flames will dance in Fenrir's eyes and leap from his nostrils. With each breath, meanwhile, Jormungand will spew venom; all the earth and the sky will be splashed and stained with his poison.

The world will be in uproar, the air quaking with booms and blares and their echoes. Then the sons of Muspell will advance from the south and tear apart the sky itself as they, too, close in on Vigrid. Surt will lead them, his sword blazing like the sun itself. And as they cross Bifrost, the rainbow bridge will crack and break behind them. So all the giants and all the dead, the monsters and the blazing sons of Muspell will gather on Vigrid; they will all but fill that plain that stretches one hundred and twenty leagues in every direction.

The gods, meanwhile, will not be idle. Heimdall will leave his hall and raise the great horn Gjall to his mouth. He will sound such a blast that it will be heard throughout the nine worlds. All the gods will wake and at once meet in council. Then Odin will mount Sleipnir and gallop to Mimir's spring and take advice from Mimir there.

Yggdrasill itself will moan, the ash that always was and waves over all that is. Its leaves will tremble, its limbs shiver and shake even as two humans take refuge deep within it. Everything in heaven and in earth and Hel will quiver.

Then all the Aesir and all the warriors in Valhalla will arm themselves. They will don their helmets and their coats of mail, and grasp their swords and spears and shields. Eight hundred fighting men will forge through each of that hall's five hundred and forty doors. That vast host will march towards Vigrid and Odin will ride at their head, wearing a golden helmet and a shining corslet, brandishing his spear Gungnir.

Odin will make straight for the wolf Fenrir; and Thor, right beside him, will be unable to help because Jormungand will at once attack him. Freyr will fight the fire giant Surt. And when Surt whirls his flaming blade, Freyr will rue the day that he gave his own good sword to his servant Skirnir. It will be a long struggle, though, before Freyr succumbs. The hound Garm will leap at the throat of one-handed Tyr and they will kill one another. Loki and Heimdall will meet in combat and each will be the cause of the other's death.

Thor and gaping Jormungand have met before too; they are well matched. At Vigrid the god will kill the serpent but he will only be able to stagger back nine steps before he falls dead himself, poisoned by the venom Jormungand spews over him.

Odin and Fenrir were the first to engage and their fight will be fearsome. In the end, though, the wolf will seize Allfather between his jaws and swallow him. That will be the death of Odin.

At once his son Vidar will stride forward and press one foot on Fenrir's bottom jaw – and the shoe he will wear then has been a long time in the making; it consists of all the strips and bits of leather pared off the heels and toes of new shoes since time began, all the leftovers thrown away as gifts for the god. Then Vidar will take hold of Fenrir's other jaw and tear the wolf apart, so avenging his father.

Then Surt will fling fire in every direction. Asgard and Midgard and Jotunheim and Niflheim will become furnaces – places of raging flame, swirling smoke, ashes, only ashes. The nine worlds will burn and the gods will die. The chosen warriors will die, men and women and children in Midgard will die, elves and dwarfs will die, giants will die, monsters and creatures of the underworld will die, birds and animals will die. The sun will be dark and there will be no stars in the sky. The earth will sink into the sea.

The earth will rise again out of the water, fair and green. The eagle will fly over cataracts, swoop into the thunder and catch fish under crags. Corn will ripen in fields that were never sown.

Vidar and Vali will still be alive; they will survive the fire and the flood and make their way back to the plain where palaces once

stood. The sons of Thor will join them there, and they will inherit
there as well, and he will hold the wand and foretell what is to come.
back from the world of the dead; it will not be long before they,
too, tread the new green grass on the shining plain. Honir will be
there as well, and he will hold the wand and foretell what is to come.

The gods in heaven, home of the winds, will sit down in the sunlight and begin to talk. Turn by turn, they will call up such memories, memories such as are known to them alone. They will talk
over many things that happened in the past, and the evil of Jormungand and the wolf Fenrir. And then, amongst the waving grass,
they will find golden chessboards, treasures owned once by the
Aesir, and gaze at them in wonder.

Many courts will rise once more, some good, some evil. The best
place of all will be Gimli in heaven, a building fairer than the sun,
roofed with gold. That is where the rulers will live, at peace with
themselves and each other. Then there will be a hall where the
ground is always warm underfoot; there will always be plenty of
good drink there for those who have a taste for it. And there will be
Sindri, a fine hall that stands in the dark mountains, made wholly of
red gold. Good men will live in these places.

But there will be another hall on the shore of corpses. That place
in the underworld will be as vile as it is vast; all its doors will face
north. Its walls and roof will be made of wattled snakes, their heads
facing inward, blowing so much poison that it runs in rivers through
the hall. Oath breakers and murderers and seducers will wade
through those rivers. The dragon Nidhogg, too, will outlive the fire
and the flood and under Yggdrasill he will suck blood from the
bodies of the dead.

The two humans who hid themselves deep within Yggdrasill will
be called Lif and Lifthrasir. Surt's fire will not scorch them; it will
not even touch them, and their food will be the morning dew.
Through the branches, through the leaves, they will see light come
back, for before the sun is caught and eaten by the wolf Skoll, she

will give birth to a daughter no less fair than herself, who will follow the same sky-path and light the world.

Lif and Lifthrasir will have children. Their children will bear children. There will be life and new life, life everywhere on earth. That was the end ; and this is the beginning.

GLOSSARY

AEGIR God of the sea. His wife is Ran and their hall is under the waves.

AESIR The race of gods who inhabit Asgard.

AFI (Grandfather) Ancestor of the race of peasants.

AI (Great Grandfather) Ancestor of the race of serfs.

ALGRON (All Green) Island where Harbard (alias Odin) stayed for five years.

ALSVID (All Swift) One of the horses that pulls the sun along her course.

ALVIS (All Knowing) Wise dwarf outwitted by Thor and turned into stone.

AMMA (Grandmother) Ancestor of the race of peasants.

ANDVARI Dwarf who owned a treasure hoard, and cursed it when it was extracted from him by Loki to pay the ransom for Otter's death.

ANGRBODA (Distress-bringer) Giantess who was the mistress of Loki and mother of Fenrir, Jormungand and Hel.

ARVAK (Early Waker) One of the horses that pulls the sun along her course.

ASGARD World of the gods.

ASK (Ash Tree) Name of the first man created by the sons of Bor.

AUDUMLA Cow created out of ice in the void Ginnungagap. She gave suck to Ymir, the first being, and then licked ice blocks into the shape of Buri, forefather of the gods.

AURVANDIL Husband of the seeress Groa. Thor made a star from his frozen toe by throwing it into the sky.

BALDER Son of Odin and Frigg. Beautiful, wise and gentle. He was killed by Hod and is to return after Ragnarok.

BAUGI Giant, brother of Suttung, who employs Odin, disguised as Bolverk, on his journey to Jotunheim to secure the mead of poetry.

BERGELMIR Only giant to escape the flood caused by dead Ymir's blood.

BERSERKS (Bear Shirts) Human warriors who went into a frenzy
    before battle and fought wearing animal skins. It was believed
    that Odin gave them special protection.
BESTLA Giantess. Wife of Bor and mother of Odin, Vili and Ve.
BIFROST Flaming three-strand rainbow bridge between Asgard and
    Midgard.
BOLVERK (Evil-doer) The name adopted by Odin on his journey
    to Jotunheim to win the mead of poetry.
BOR Son of Buri, and father of Odin, Vili and Ve.
BRISINGS' NECKLACE Incomparable necklace worn by Freyja.
BROKK Dwarf who, with his brother Eitri, fashioned three such
    gifts for the gods that he won a wager with Loki.
BURI Ancestor of the gods licked from the ice by the cow Audumla.
DAY Son of Night and Delling. He rides round the world on his
    horse Skinfaxi.
DRAUPNIR (Dropper) Odin's gold ring that produces eight rings
    of equal weight on every ninth night.
DVALIN Dwarf who was turned to stone by the sun. The dwarfs
    ironically called the sun 'Dvalin's delight'.
EDDA (Great-grandmother) Ancestor of the race of serfs.
EITRI Dwarf. Brother of Brokk. He was a master-smith who
    fashioned three great gifts for the gods.
ELIVAGAR (Stormy Waves) Eleven rivers that flow from the spring
    Hvergelmir in Niflheim.
ELLI (Old Age) Old woman who wrestled with Thor in the court of
    Utgard-Loki.
EMBLA (Elm Tree) Name of the first woman created by the sons of
    Bor from a fallen tree.
FAFNIR Son of the farmer-magician Hreidmar and brother of Otter.
FATHIR (Father) Ancestor of the nobly born.
FENRIR Wolf, son of Loki, who is bound by the gods and will
    remain so until Ragnarok, the end of the world.
FIMBULVETR The terrible winter, three years in duration, that will
    precede Ragnarok.
FJALAR Dwarf. Brother of Galar and, with him, murderer of the
    wise Kvasir from whose blood they make the mead of poetry.
FJALAR Cock that will crow to warn the giants when Ragnarok, the
    end of the world, is at hand.
FRANANG'S FALLS Waterfall in Midgard in which Loki disguised
    as a salmon is caught by the gods.
FREYJA Foremost goddess of fertility. Sister of Freyr.

FREYR Foremost god of fertility.

FRIGG Odin's wife and first among the goddesses. Mother of Balder.

GALAR Dwarf. Brother of Fjalar and, with him, murderer of the wise Kvasir from whose blood they make the mead of poetry.

GARM Hound chained in the cave at the entrance to Niflheim. He will break loose at Ragnarok and kill, and be killed by, the war god Tyr.

GEFION (Giver) A fertility goddess especially connected with the plough who tricked the King of Sweden out of a tract of his kingdom – the modern Zealand.

GEIRROD Giant who tried to kill Thor.

GERD (Field) Frost giantess whose beauty ravished Freyr. He finally married her.

GILLING Giant. He and his wife are murdered by the dwarfs Fjalar and Galar. They are avenged by their son Suttung.

GIMLI Hall which will be inhabited by the ruling gods in the world after Ragnarok.

GINNUNGAGAP (Seeming Emptiness) Void that existed between Muspell and Niflheim before the creation.

GJALL (Ringing Horn) Horn of the god Heimdall which can be heard throughout the nine worlds.

GJALP (Howler) Daughter of the giant Geirrod who tried to crush Thor against roof rafters.

GLADSHEIM (Place of Joy) Sanctuary of the gods on the plain of Ida in which Odin and the principal gods had high seats.

GLEIPNIR Magic fetter made by the dwarfs and used by the gods to bind the wolf Fenrir.

GOLD MANE Hrungnir's horse, renowned for its speed.

GREIP (Grasper) Daughter of the giant Geirrod and sister of Gjalp.

GRID Giantess who was a mistress of Odin and assisted Thor by lending him her magic gloves, girdle and staff with which to defend himself against the giant Geirrod.

GROA Seeress who tried to remove whetstone fragments from Thor's head. Wife of Aurvandil.

GULLINBURSTI (Golden-bristled) Golden boar made by two dwarfs for Loki to give to the god Freyr.

GUNGNIR Odin's magic spear, forged by the dwarfs called the sons of Ivaldi.

GUNNLOD Daughter of the giant Suttung and guardian of the mead of poetry. Odin seduced her and won the mead.

GYLFI King of Sweden who is tricked by the goddess Gefion.

GYMIR Frost Giant. Father of the giantess Gerd who marries Freyr.

HARBARD (Grey-beard) Ferryman who wrangles with Thor. He is in fact Odin in disguise.

HATI Wolf who pursues the moon and will swallow it before Ragnarok.

HEAVEN BELLOWER One of Hymir's oxen. Thor used its head as bait.

HEIMDALL God who was the son of nine mothers. Owner of the horn Gjall and watchman of the gods. He disguises himself as Rig to create the three races of man.

HEL Daughter of Loki. A monster, half alive and half dead who rules the realm of the dead which is also called Hel.

HEL Realm of the dead, in Niflheim, presided over by the monster Hel.

HERMOD Son of Odin who rode to Hel to bring back his brother Balder.

HLESEY (Island of Hler) Island near which the gods Aegir and Ran lived in their hall under the sea.

HLIDSKJALF (Hill-opening or Rock-opening) Odin's high seat in Valaskjalf from which he could survey all that happened in the nine worlds.

HNITBJORG The giant Suttung's mountain stronghold where he hid the mead of poetry.

HOD Blind god who unwittingly killed his own brother Balder. He will return after Ragnarok.

HONIR Long-legged god known for indecisiveness. He will survive Ragnarok.

HRAESVELG (Corpse Eater) Giant disguised as eagle who causes the wind.

HREIDMAR Farmer and magician. Father of Otter, Fafnir and Regin who acquired a ransom with a curse on it from Odin, Honir and Loki.

HRUNGNIR Strongest of the giants. He lost a horse race with Odin and was subsequently killed in a duel with Thor.

HUGI (Thought) Young giant who outstripped Thor's human servant Thialfi in a running race and was, in fact, the embodiment of Utgard-Loki's thought.

HVERGELMIR Spring in Niflheim under one root of Yggdrasill. The eleven rivers called the Elivigar spring from it.

HYMIR Giant. His massive cauldron required by the gods for the brewing of ale was wrested from him by Thor who subsequently killed him.

HYRROKIN Giantess who drags Balder's burial boat, Ringhorn, down to the sea.

IDAVOLL (Field of Deeds) Central plain in Asgard, site of Gladsheim and Vingolf, the halls where the principal gods and goddesses met in council.

IDUN Goddess and custodian of the golden apples of youth.

IVALDI Two dwarfs called the 'sons of Ivaldi' make three great treasures for the gods.

IVING River that divides Asgard from Jotunheim. It never freezes.

JARL (Earl or Nobly-born) The god Heimdall claimed him as his son and taught him the runes and their meaning.

JORMUNGAND Serpent, offspring of Loki and Angrboda. He encircles Midgard and bites on his own tail. Also called the 'Midgard Serpent'.

JOTUNHEIM Realm of the giants.

KARL (Churl) Ancestor of the race of peasants.

KON (King) Son of Jarl whom the god Heimdall claimed as his son. He learned the runes and could understand the speech of birds.

KVASIR A wise man created from the spittle of the gods. Murdered by two dwarfs, the mead of poetry was brewed from his blood.

LIF (Life) Man who will hide in Yggdrasill, survive Ragnarok, and father children to repeople the earth.

LIFTHRASIR (Eager for life) Woman who will hide in Yggdrasill, survive Ragnarok, and mother children to repeople the earth.

LIT Dwarf cremated with Balder and Nanna.

LOGI (Flames) Fire in the form of a giant who beat Loki in an eating match at the court of Utgard-Loki.

LOKI Attractive, ambivalent, mischief-making god (the son of two giants). Often called the Sly One, the Trickster, the Shape Changer, the Sky Traveller. He grows progressively more evil, causes the death of Balder, and is bound until the coming of Ragnarok, the end of the world.

MAGNI (Might) Son of Thor and the giantess Jarnsaxa (Iron Cutlass). He and his brother Modi will inherit the hammer Mjollnir after Ragnarok.

MIDGARD (Middle World) The world of men.

MIMIR'S WELL Well of wisdom under the root of Yggdrasill in Jotunheim, protected by the head of Mimir.

MIST CALF Giant made of clay, nine leagues tall. An ineffectual companion for the giant Hrungnir in his duel against Thor.

MJOLLNIR Thor's hammer, made by the dwarfs Brokk and Eitri. Symbol of destruction, fertility (used to hallow brides at weddings) and resurrection (Thor brings his goats back to life with it).

MOON Son of Mundilfari. He drives the moon on its course and determines its waxing and waning.

MOTHIR (Mother) Ancestor of the nobly born.

MUNDILFARI (Turner) Human father of Moon and Sun.

MUSPELL Realm of fire in the south, guarded by the giant Surt. The fusion of its heat with Niflheim's ice led to the creation.

MUSPELL, SONS OF Fire giants who will fight under the giant Surt at Ragnarok.

NANNA Balder's wife.

NARVI Loki's son by his wife Sigyn. He was killed by his own brother Vali and Loki was bound with his entrails.

NIDHOGG (Corpse Tearer) Dragon that gnaws at the roots of Yggdrasill in Niflheim and chews corpses.

NIFLHEIM A realm of freezing mist and darkness under one root of Yggdrasill. Hel lies within it.

NIGHT Daughter of Narvi. Mother of Day. She rides her horse Hrimfaxi round the world.

NJORD One of the fertility gods and father of Freyr and Freyja. Associated with the wind and sea.

NORNS The three goddesses of destiny, Urd (Fate), Skuld (Being) and Verdandi (Necessity).

ODIN Father of Thor and first and foremost of the Aesir. God of Poetry, Battle and Death. He has many names amongst which are Allfather, God of Gods, the Terrible One, One-eyed, Father of Battle, the Raider.

OTTER Son of the farmer-magician Hreidmar. He was killed by Loki, and Odin, Honir and Loki paid a ransom of red gold to his father as compensation.

RAGNAROK (Destruction of the Powers). The apocalyptic final battle between the gods and the giants, involving all creation, in which virtually all life is destroyed and the nine worlds are submerged.

RAN Wife of Aegir, god of the sea. She dragged drowning men down with a net.

REGIN Son of the farmer-magician Hreidmar and brother of Otter and Fafnir.

RIG (King) The name assumed by the god Heimdall when he created the three races of men.

RIND Goddess. Mistress of Odin. Their son was Vali.

RINGHORN Balder's boat in which he and his wife Nanna were cremated.

ROSKVA Farmer's daughter and sister of Thialfi who becomes servant of Thor. She accompanied Thor on his great expedition to Utgard.

SIF Thor's wife whose golden hair was cut off by Loki. The dwarfs spun a skein to replace it.

SIGYN Loki's faithful wife.

SINDRI Hall in the world to come after Ragnarok with a roof of red gold.

SKIDBLADNIR (Wooden-bladed) Collapsible ship. One of the three precious objects made by the sons of the dwarf Ivaldi for Freyr.

SKIRNIR (Shining) Freyr's messenger who won the giantess Gerd for him.

SKOLL Wolf that pursues the sun and will swallow it before Ragnarok.

SKRYMIR (Big Bloke) Extra large giant (in fact Utgard-Loki in disguise) encountered by Thor and his companions on their journey to Utgard.

SLEIPNIR Odin's eight-legged horse. He was sired by the stallion Svadilfari and borne by Loki.

SNÖR Ancestress of the race of peasants.

SUN Daughter of Mundilfari. She drives the sun on its course.

SURT (Black) The giant who has guarded Muspell (the realm of fire) since before the creation. He will set fire to the world at Ragnarok.

SUTTUNG Giant. Son of the giant Gilling. For some time custodian of the mead of poetry.

SVADILFARI Stallion that assists the giant mason to build the walls of Asgard. Father of Sleipnir, Odin's eight-legged horse.

THIALFI Farmer's son who becomes Thor's servant. Immensely fleet of foot but outstripped by Hugi ('Thought') in a running race at the court of Utgard-Loki.

THIAZI Giant. He stole the goddess Idun and the golden apples in her keeping but Loki retrieved them and Thiazi was killed by the gods.

THIR (Drudge) Human wife of Thrall.

THOKK Giantess, probably Loki in disguise, who prevented Balder's return from Hel.

THOR Son of Odin and Earth, and husband of Sif. Second in the hierarchy of the gods and their guardian. God of the sky and thunder and so of fertility but equally associated with maintenance of law and order in Midgard. The most common of his many names are Thunder God and Hurler and Charioteer.

THRALL Human. Son of Ai and Edda. Husband of Thir.

THRUD (Might) Daughter of Thor, promised by the gods to the dwarf Alvis.

THRYM Giant, described as King of the frost giants. He stole Thor's hammer and paid for it with his life.

THRYMHEIM (Place of Din) The giant Thiazi's stronghold in the mountains.

TYR God of war. Son of Odin (or possibly the giant Hymir). The bravest of the gods who sacrificed one hand so that the wolf Fenrir could be bound.

URD (Fate) One of the three Norns or goddesses of destiny. The Well of Urd, which they guard, lies under the root of Yggdrasill in Asgard. The gods held a daily assembly there.

UTGARD Stronghold within Jotunheim, ruled by the giant king Utgard-Loki.

UTGARD-LOKI Ruler of Utgard and a master of illusion who outwits Thor and his companions.

VALI Son of Loki and his wife Sigyn. The gods turned him into a wolf and he killed his own brother Narvi.

VALI Son of Odin and his giant mistress Rind expressly conceived to take vengeance for his half-brother Balder's death.

VALASKJALF (Shelf of the slain) Odin's hall in Asgard.

VALHALLA (Hall of the Slain) Immense hall, presided over by Odin, where the Einherjar (dead warriors) fought, feasted, and awaited Ragnarok, the final destruction.

VALKYRIES (Choosers of the Slain) Beautiful young women who chose men doomed to die in battle and brought them back to Valhalla.

VANIR A race of fertility gods who became integrated with the Aesir after the great battle mentioned at the beginning of the second myth.

VAR (Oath) Goddess who hears marriage oaths and punishes those who do not keep them.

VE Son of Bor and brother of Odin and Vili.

VEUR The name taken by Thor when he visited the giant Hymir.

VIDAR Son of Odin and the giantess Grid who will avenge Odin's death and survive Ragnarok.

VIGRID (Battle Shaker) Vast plain in Asgard on which the final battle between gods and men, giants and monsters will take place.

VILI Son of Bor and brother of Odin and Ve.

VINGOLF Hall in Asgard in which the goddesses had their high seats.

YGGDRASILL (The Terrible One's Horse) The World Tree, an ash that linked and sheltered all the worlds.

YMIR The first giant, formed from fire and ice. The world was shaped out of his body.

293
CR

Crossley-Holland,
Kevin

Axe-age, wolf-age

$11.95

DATE		